ACHIEVING REAL HAPPINESS

ACHIEVING REAL HAPPINESS

By Kenneth Hildebrand

HARPER & BROTHERS PUBLISHERS NEW YORK

TO SARAH AND KENNY

who already
have given joy that they know not of
and who, with life before them,
have yet to discover that
happiness nestles at the bottom of the barrel

CONTENTS

INTRODUCTION

YEARS ago a skeptical student sat occasionally in the back
pew of the church on Sunday. He was fumbling for something in which to invest his abilities, something to tie his life
together, to grant meaning and personal happiness. But he
was skeptical of religion. Too many clergymen seemed second rate, too many questions remained unanswered, too
many churchmen fell short of their affirmations. Religion as
taught and preached seemed vague, sentimental and unrealistic. The student in the back pew matched wits with the
man in the pulpit and mentally challenged the assertions the
preacher made. Cynicism bested yearning. Religion was not
practical, he decided; it had little to do with the gritty affairs
of life.

I was that student. Later something happened—or, more
correctly, a number of influences converged on my life—and
eventually I found myself the man in the pulpit. The perspective was different, but the initial concern did not change.
The conviction deepened that religious faith, insight and expression must be germane to the business of living here and
now, or it loses its primary value. Certain theologians may
disagree, but this is my settled opinion. "I am come," said
the Master of living, "that they might have life, and that
they might have it more abundantly." I have not forgotten
that skeptical young man challenging the preacher's state-
ments from the rear row and, according to my ability, I have
striven to present to him a straightforward, realistic faith. Is
religion practical? *So practical that in this complex, muddled
world it is impossible to live from any depth of being without*

it! In a sense, this book springs from my respect and concern for the questioning man in the pew—or the one who would occupy the pew if he sensed that religion and competent living have vital commerce with each other.

Yet what I have written is not a special pleading for religious faith. Deliberately I have made effort to avoid that. A wise counselor, I believe, begins with people at their level of spiritual understanding, not at his own; his attitude is not "Thus saith the Lord" but "How understandest thou?" However, as he deals with their needs and difficulties, sooner or later religion imposes itself. This is not through devious or deliberate manipulation; it is because the questions that torment mankind are spiritual questions. The bald fact is that troubled souls need that which genuine religious faith can produce. As Steinmetz has said, "Some day people will learn that material things do not bring happiness and are of little use in making men and women creative and powerful. Then the scientists of the world will turn their laboratories over to the study of God and prayer and the spiritual forces which, as yet, have been hardly scratched. When that day comes, the world will see more advancement in one generation than it has seen in the last four."

If the evangelical note seems muted in these pages, it is not because it is unimportant. The above considerations dictate the lack of emphasis, coupled with the fact that the book is not directed to theologians. It is centered in the individual who, in the stress of life, seeks serviceable tools to help him understand and stabilize himself. I trust, also, that what is written may be of some assistance to clergymen as they minister to the perturbed persons who seek their counsel.

A friend who writes radio and television commercials once explained to me his vivid mental picture of the consumer to whom he must appeal. He did not write to a vague mass of people, he said, but to a specific potential customer, a woman, a composite of the individuals whom he hoped to reach. This imaginary person was real to him. He knew her age, size, nationality, and the coloring of her hair and eyes. He knew her home, her neighborhood, how many children she had and what her income was. He knew her likes and dislikes, her worries, problems, friends, education and religious beliefs. He even had given her a name!

The person to whom I have written is almost as vivid to me. I say almost, for again and again the composite shifts and I see real persons and living faces. The perplexities I describe, the fears and frustrations, the achievements and adjustments are theirs, although I have taken care to guard their anonymity.

My composite individual is modern, urbane, competent and probably successful by ordinary standards. He—or she— is above average in education and mental alertness. He has friends and enjoys being appreciated, but does not always put his best foot forward. He believes in a Supreme Being, holds respect for the church or synagogue and attends services at least occasionally. Probably he was reared in a religious home; he may complain that religion was "crammed down his throat" when he was young. He has a realistic turn of mind that likes to weigh the evidence and does not accept dogmatic assertions easily. Frankly, religion thus far has offered little practical help in meeting his personal problems.

And he has problems, although on the surface they may not be evident. Some of them are objective enough—his business, his home, his children, his frustrations, his health. Other problems are not as concrete, but prove even more baffling. Some stem from an ill-defined feeling of dissatisfaction; life does not have the zest it should; he has not found the happiness that he feels he has a right to expect. Living gets complicated and confused; he worries too much, keeps himself busy to avoid emptiness, and questions the purpose of it all. He cannot understand himself in many instances—why he acts or feels as he does, why he is filled with insecurity, why he becomes depressed, or why a sense of guilt plagues him. It is my hope that the pages following will help this person to a clearer self-understanding, a better adjustment to existence, and to the discovery of attitudes, habits and resources that can aid him in achieving real happiness.

"None of us liveth to himself and no man dieth to himself" —nor does one write a book of himself. My bundle of gratitude is larger than these pages can contain. The saints and seers whose wisdom has lighted a flame to which we still may bring our faggots; the gallant souls, confronting drudgery and disaster with faith and steady courage, who wist not that their faces shone; the mentors, friends, instructors and companions; the people who in plenty and in want, in joy and in sorrow, in sickness and in health, have dealt with me kindly along the path of experience and who have shared with me far more than they themselves have received; those who have loved me too much to let me go unchastened and yet have inspired me to fresh endeavors; and little children who make old things new and new things wonderful—how can one thank such a company?

In the specific preparation of this book, I acknowledge gratefully my indebtedness to Mr. and Mrs. Alfred L. Mell, whose assistance and encouragement engineered the publication of the manuscript from "sometime" into "now"; to Mrs. R. Winfield Ellis, who suggested the idea around which these pages developed and who has given invaluable counsel and criticism; to Harold A. Belt and Norman F. Barry for their wise and stimulating advice; and to Nell Hildebrand, whose common sense has anchored flights of fancy to the rock of reality. I am under special obligation to Beryl D.

Orris, M.D., Ph.D., who has shared with me his insights into many personality problems and has offered valued suggestions relative to portions of the book. Finally, I extend heartfelt appreciation to Mrs. Maude Joannes for the preparation of the manuscript, and to Mrs. William H. Stevenson for typing numerous sections.

KENNETH HILDEBRAND

The Central Church
Chicago, Illinois

ACHIEVING REAL HAPPINESS

CHAPTER I

Introduction to Happiness

OUR generation yearns for happiness. Observe the throngs at night swarming to the heart of any city in search of amusement. Consider the millions of dollars spent annually to purchase pleasure. Look into your own heart to discover how deeply you desire a sincere sense of satisfaction and a lasting contentment. All signs point to a thirst for happiness.

Yet note the sullen and unhappy facial expressions of those we meet. Sense the spirit of unrest and dissatisfaction in those with whom we associate. Read the newspaper accounts of what people do out of sheer boredom. At times we are tempted to wonder if to be genuinely happy is regarded as a crime! Certainly happiness escapes a startling number of persons. Yet, on the other hand, there are others whose presence is both a stimulus and a benediction. Poised and dynamic, they attract by a compelling radiance and *joie de vivre*. Why should this be so? How does it happen that they discover personal serenity while others seem unable ever to do so? How is it that some lives are like springs from which joy and laughter bubble continuously, while other personalities resemble dry cisterns? Their laughter is too strident, their voices too shrill and their response to pleasure either forced or blasé. Perhaps those who fail to find happiness are confused as to what happiness is; they search for it where it does not dwell.

Let us assure ourselves, first of all, that our desire for happiness is valid and reasonable. It is not a shimmering mirage, a consummation devoutly to be wished but utterly unobtainable. It is not something to which we have no right. Happiness is the normal state of every individual, just as health rather than illness is the normal state of the body. "If a man is unhappy," wrote Epictetus, a slave in Nero's Rome, "remember that his unhappiness is his own fault, for God made all men to be happy." [1] The proof that happiness is both normal and good lies in the results it produces; happiness *works*. Like a machine perfectly balanced and in tune, with each component part moving with highest efficiency, so we function with greatest ease when we are happy; it is then we generate our greatest power. We have more energy, produce finer results with less effort, get along better with others and live with greater zest. Happiness enables us to give ourselves wholeheartedly to whatever we do—to absorb ourselves in our work, our pleasures, or our interest in others; to relax more completely, to feel that whatever we are doing is an expression of ourselves. Such harmony and well-being mean more to us than the social or financial rewards that may accrue to our efforts. One man said, "Sometimes it hardly seems right to accept my salary. I have so much fun in my work that I'd pay for the chance to do it." Any truly happy person understands what he meant.

Since happiness is normal, each of us can be happy. Like health, however, certain laws must be observed—which shall be discussed in the pages ahead—and happiness results, as surely as two plus two equals four, or that daylight follows the rising sun.

Unhappiness, like alcoholism or chronic fear, is not a sudden development. The unhappy state is preceded by a long tragic history of destructive attitudes and negative thoughts; of engrossing self-concern and selfish actions; of unrealistic self-appraisal and unhealthy relationship with others; of refusal to acquire habits and skills essential to self-confidence and objectivity; of nursing resentments and bitterness; and of coddled emotional immaturities. If chronic unhappiness plagues our lives, we are guilty of such malpractices, no matter how unwittingly. The critical question then becomes: *What can we do to overcome our deficiencies and to discover a permanent sense of happiness?* The task is by no means impossible.

Consider some of the reasons for our failure to gain inner satisfactions. First, in our frantic search for happiness we assume it resides in *something that we can possess or manipulate:* a spacious home, smart clothes, powerful automobiles or a huge bank account; we think of expensive vacations or costly amusements. We are sorely mistaken. If we have material comforts and at the same time possess happiness, it means that our happiness stems from within ourselves. It resides in something we *are,* not in what we *have.* "I am convinced from experience," wrote Henry David Thoreau in *Walden,* "that to maintain oneself on this earth is not a hardship but a pastime, if we will live simply and wisely. . . . Most of the luxuries, and many of the so-called comforts of life, are not only dispensable, but positive hindrances to the elevation of mankind."

In Lewis Carroll's *Through the Looking Glass,* Alice meets the White Knight. He is cumbered with contraptions—a beehive to capture a vagrant swarm of bees, a mouse trap to make short work of a molesting rodent, anklets around his horse's feet to protect against sharks, and a dish in anticipation of the plum pudding that some kind soul might offer him. Laden with gadgets, the White Knight is a symbol of all misguided people who seek happiness by accumulating things.

Yet the conviction persists that possessions and wealth command happiness. A magazine survey revealed lack of

money as the chief cause of unhappiness. If one had money enough, people maintained, one could buy happiness. The fallacy of such belief is recorded endlessly. A wealthy young cattleman, for instance, owner of a 2500-acre ranch, took his private plane into the sky early one morning and then radioed his family he would dive to his death when the fuel was exhausted. Frantically those on the ground tried to dissuade him, reminding him of his wife, his three-year-old daughter, and that his wife was expecting another child in six weeks. "Everything is all messed up," he replied. "I just can't face it." His family knew of no trouble and pleaded with him to land the plane safely. Stubbornly he insisted that life was too great a burden. Finally his plane screamed from a height of ten thousand feet and crashed into a gravel pit. Surrounded by wealth, comfort and love, with wide opportunity before him, he decided that he just couldn't face it.

The calypso tune that flashed for its moment of popularity put it succinctly:

> The poor man, he would give his soul
> If only he had the rich man's gold.
> The rich man, he would give all his wealth
> If only he had the poor man's health.[2]

Marcus Aurelius, the Roman philosopher, observed: "Thou seest how few things are needful for man to live a happy and godlike life: for, if he observe these, heaven will demand no more."[3] Genuine happiness is hidden in the quiet simplicities and fundamental virtues of life; these cannot be purchased, even though one could afford to pay a king's ransom.

Another popular fallacy is that happiness hinges on *pleasant circumstances and congenial surroundings*. Many believe that, if their situations were altered, their cares would forsake them. "Fate is against me," they complain. "How can I be happy, surrounded as I am by disagreeable duties? See the difficulties I face and the people with whom I deal. Notice how distasteful and monotonous my life has become. If only I could change my circumstances, I could be supremely happy!" Granted that the impact of circumstances can shake our lives to the roots, happiness does not depend on them; it can be a reality in spite of circumstances.

A woman, for example, was married to a cruel, shiftless, alcoholic man. When drunk he would beat her and the children. Debts accumulated. Often there was no food in the house. When the oldest child was seven, the husband deserted his wife. She had no money, no credit and no business training. She underwent surgery, thus adding to her mountain of debt. A few months later the youngest child became ill and died. When the father received the news by wire, he telegraphed in reply, "Terrible shock. Sorry to hear the news." His heartlessness so angered the woman that she resolved to rear the children without him at whatever cost to herself.

The following nine years she toiled at any work available. She never lost her determination or her sense of humor, and prided herself in not saying or doing anything to turn the children against their father. She managed to keep the home together and to make it a cheery one. At the end of nine years she married a man who loved her and the children devotedly.

To encourage other women undergoing difficult experiences, she said, "Any woman can wring happiness out of life if she is worthy of happiness." Her words are worth remembering. Her well-being did not depend on circumstances. She was superior to them.

When we allow surroundings and situations to dictate the degree of our unhappiness, we are making excuse for a spirit of dissatisfaction that we have permitted to grow. Perhaps we have concentrated on small matters, have majored in irritations and minored in understanding, and have permitted envy and ill-will to distort our view. Thus, by the unhealthy patterns we have developed, we have imposed unhappiness on ourselves. Nearly eight hundred years ago St. Bernard declared, "Nothing can work me damage except myself; the harm that I sustain I carry with me, and I am the real sufferer by my own fault." Through our personal attitudes we select joy or dissatisfaction, happiness or gloom. We choose to be worthy of happiness, or we sentence ourselves to unhappiness. Outward circumstances cannot steal our serenity if we will it otherwise. The most radiant personalities, whose happiness comes from the greatest depth of being, are among those who have risen above adverse circumstances. Difficulty can provide the flame to temper the cutting edge of our spirits.

Nor does happiness come through *ignoring the misery and suffering in the world.* Some persons attempt to insure personal happiness by swathing themselves in comforts and by closing their eyes to suffering. They endeavor to isolate themselves in sterile ivory towers where none of the germs of human agony can infect them. By ignoring pain and misery, they hope to avoid them. But theirs is a losing effort; it is impossible to ignore human misery completely. A century ago, people did not worry about starving multitudes in a distant corner of the earth, or shudder at the horrors of a plague across the seas. By the time the news of such catastrophes reached them, it was too late to help. Today we are not similarly insulated. The ills of the world storm our breakfast tables. Newspapers, radio and television hurl the brutal facts at us. In a world as closely related as ours, the despairing cry of a hungry peasant in Asia or of a native in Africa reverberates until its thunder smashes against the walls of peace we have carefully constructed. Human need is a reality. A deep satisfaction comes when we open our hearts to the suffering in the world and do what we can to alleviate it.

Another difficulty in our quest for happiness is that *we confuse happiness with pleasure.* We assume they are synonymous, but a vast gulf separates them. Pleasure is an agreeable sensation or emotion, while happiness is a basic state or quality of life. Happiness is much deeper and more fundamental, and therefore the more satisfying. It is possible to enjoy a pleasure relating only remotely to happiness, even as one can experience happiness in which there is little or no pleasure.

Happiness, for example, can result from sacrifice. In England, after World War II, a memorial tablet was dedicated to three British women, commemorating their heroism and sacrifice.[4] All three had served as secret agents in occupied France. One was forty years of age, another twenty-six and the third only twenty-three. Each was captured, one was tortured and all were executed. What they endured in their hazardous work did not give them pleasure; there was no enjoyment in hardship, imprisonment and death. Yet each experienced a fundamental joy that lies at the heart of loyalty and sacrifice.

In George Eliot's *Romula,* the mother considers with her little son the investment of his life. He says he wants to choose something that will allow him a great deal of pleasure. Looking into her own tragic past, she tells him, "The best happiness is that which comes with thinking much about other people, and that often brings so much pain with it that we can only tell it from pain by its being what we would choose above everything else because our souls see that it is good." In some forms of happiness the element of pleasure is almost nonexistent. But they are forms of happiness, nonetheless, often of the purest kind.

Thus happiness is not synonymous with pleasure. It does

not depend on external things, favorable circumstances, or freedom from pain. Like a nightingale, happiness can sing sweetly in the dark.

Still another reason why happiness eludes us is that *we pursue it too aggressively*. In almost everything we undertake, success depends on effort, attack, persistence and the output of energy. We assume that happiness is similarly won. It proves an exception to the rule, however. Effort and striving do not bring us closer to this coveted goal. Once, on a vacation trip, our daughter found a bedraggled kitten. Her heart went out to the pitiful creature and she begged to take it home. Reluctantly we granted permission. She named the kitten Happy, perhaps as a challenge. In one sense, Happy lived up to her name. Whenever we wanted her and tried to catch her, she skillfully eluded us. If we ignored her and went about our duties, soon she was purring at our feet.

Happiness is not captured by frontal attack; when we lay aside our arms and renounce the campaign, it stands at our side. Happiness comes by indirection. Not sensing this, but determined to overwhelm it by force, we find ourselves resembling the woman who took a little girl to the circus. She wanted the little girl to have a good time, but the child never had been to the circus before and it was big, strange and bewildering. The queer sights and sounds, the noise and the excitement frightened her. Finally, in exasperation, the woman shook her roughly and demanded, "I brought you here to have a good time. Now go ahead and have it!"

We say to ourselves, "I *am* going to be happy!" We grasp ourselves by the nape of the neck, so to speak, shake ourselves thoroughly and demand, "Now go ahead and be happy!" But happiness does not respond to such treatment. It is always a by-product. We lay aside our relentless quest for happiness, apply ourselves elsewhere—and suddenly we find it nestled in our breasts. It comes as a gift, not by the right of conquest or as a salary that we have a right to demand. Like the old lady who searched everywhere for the spectacles she thought she had lost before finding them on the end of her nose, we discover happiness close at hand.

The source of happiness, then, in common with the springs of all that is good or evil, *lies within ourselves*. Externals—the circumstances under which we live and labor, the state of our health, our material comfort, the fulfillment of our desires—have a bearing on our immediate responses and influence them toward dismay or a sense of well-being. But the externals of life are not gods, whimsically ordaining happiness or unhappiness; our personal destinies are not in the hands of such caprice. Something within us can conquer circumstance, something with power to climb the dark mountains of difficulty and to face hostile happenings with steady eyes. It is what we bring to existence that counts supremely, not what life flings at us.

To this point, basically we have considered what happiness is *not*. But negative knowledge is an insufficient foundation on which to build a happy existence. A positive dynamic must motivate the truly happy individual. Although it is difficult to capture the intrinsic nature of happiness in a cage of words, it is essential to arrive at a workable definition. *Happiness is wholeness of personality*. Wholeness is a feeling of rapport and "at homeness" in the world. It is a state of mental health in the widest, most constructive sense; it is a mark of maturity. Wholeness is a feeling of adequacy for existence. To be whole—in a right relationship with ourselves, with others, with existence and with the universe—is to be happy.

Wholeness, and therefore happiness essential and intrinsic elements: it d unity, a sense of meaning and a feeling

First, in the search for happiness then

We are made to invest ourselves in something outside our-selves, something that concentrates our lives into a funda-mental unity, gives meaning to our struggles and heartaches, and rewards us with inner peace. The deepest satisfactions escape us until we do. Such allegiance does for our interests and energies what a magnet does with disorganized steel filings—pulls them together, unifies them into a pattern, gives them soundness and direction. When we center our personal-ities around satisfying objectives, we are no longer at civil war within, with our various impulses tugging helter-skelter, our desires at swords' points, and our energies diffused; we are all in one piece. Life's external trappings do not have the power to grant such a royal gift. Whatever commands our loyalty serves to co-ordinate our inner powers and to turn us toward completeness. Such unity starts when we can say, "I belong to *that!*"

It must not be overlooked, however, that the goals to which we give allegiance are of varied worth. Some values stand high in their ethical and moral effect on personality, while others are low or even dangerous. Hitler, for instance, unified his energies around objectives low in the moral scale; the result plunged the world into chaos and his name into infamy. It is possible to consolidate life around a lust for money, sex or material possessions; to thirst for adulation or coarse pleasures. The integration on such low levels maims or denies essential drives in human personality and thus leaves a man incomplete and dissatisfied, convinced that somehow life has managed to cheat him. The fault does not lie in the outgoing allegiance, but in the objects around which he seeks compactness. Life at its happiest selects goals of exacting worth, adequate to call forth the best qualities within.

Also, before there can be adequate integration of person-ality with its resultant happiness, there must be *a sense of meaning* to make the struggle for oneness and inner peace seem worth while. Meaning is the second essential in wholeness of personality. The diffused and unhappy person becomes pessimistic about the ultimate sense of life and takes a dim view of his own significance. "Why should I agonize to change myself?" he asks. "Why should I strive to organize my life around anything? What lasting good can it accomplish? My life doesn't mean much, anyway."

Fresh incentives must revitalize such a person to a new interest in life if he is to tackle seriously the problem of his own integration. A business executive who quit a thirty thousand dollar a year job to accept a five thousand dollar teaching position, explained, "After all, life should represent something more than the ability to make money"—such conviction would do it. William Lloyd Garrison, abolitionist leader, when subjected to threats and violence, declared, "I am in earnest. I will not equivocate; I will not excuse; I will not retreat a single inch; and I will be heard!"—such a sense of purpose would achieve it. He who finds no sustaining meaning in life urgently needs to discover goals which in their importance to him far outweigh whatever struggle he must undergo to attain them.

The problem is complicated further by the unhealthy personality pattern that the disorganized individual has followed. Undoubtedly he has been engrossed in himself, bending all his energies and interests inward. Like a painting in which all lines converge on a single spot, he has placed his ego at the focal center of attention. So far as he is concerned, the world takes meaning only in relation to himself; in his own eyes he is supremely important. He views others through the spectacles of self-esteem and sees them, not as kindred beings, but as instruments to forward his personal ambitions and desires—pawns to use for his own selfish ends, or props to bolster his emotional insecurity. Eventually he has difficulty in maintaining a balanced relationship with others, or even in evaluating himself correctly.

He may struggle to free himself from self-concern, realizing its dangers. Normally he attempts to do so by exercising will power. Even as he strives to center his attention on outward events, he keeps a vigilant eye on himself to see that he does so. In reality, he is in the position of the frontiersmen who listened to an unscrupulous magician who traveled from village to village, proclaiming that he could turn base metals into gold. With elaborate flourishes he stirred a mixture while he chanted a magic formula. Without being observed he dropped in a gold nugget which, when he poured off the brew, remained for all to see. As greedy onlookers offered to buy his secret, he drew them aside one by one, extracted his fee, and gave them the mysterious formula. Then he would say with deep impressiveness, "As you stir the chemicals and pronounce the magic words, you must *never* think of a yellow apple the color of the gold you want to appear in the pan. If you do, you will spoil everything!" The victims never found gold; they always thought of a yellow apple!

Determined to surmount self-concern through will power, the unhappy individual faces a similar dilemma. Since what he thinks and does still actually revolves around himself, his struggles serve only to deepen his ego-centeredness. Sensing that it is a losing game, his despair and unhappiness increase.

In order to live happily with ourselves, there must be room for sincere self-expression, the discovery of rich values, and the achievement of enduring satisfactions. Existence must have *meaning*. The selfish individual tries to build on too slender a base. It is like trying to balance the White House on top of the Washington Monument; the attempt is doomed to failure. It may take time for the egocentric structure of personality to topple; indeed, it may continue throughout life. But the end result is inevitable. When all avenues in a person's life lead toward himself, with no return traffic of kindly deeds or generous thoughts to counterbalance the flow of incoming blessings, there can be no result except unhappiness. Those who demand that life cater to them finally find that life is dissatisfying—although they may not have the remotest notion why. Even ill health may result. As competent physicians have observed, both the mental and physical health of a person may be gauged by the extent to which his interests move in circles outside himself.

The Japanese have a way of stunting a tree by tying off the taproot so that the tree remains a miniature of the forest giant it could have been. In similar fashion, we dwarf our lives by tying off the taproots which feed an ever-widening list of objective interests. Thus we deny ourselves the satisfaction which our lives crave.

A man whose wife was inclined to self-centeredness died suddenly, leaving half of his estate to her and half to various nieces and nephews. Without exception the latter spent the money lavishly until it was gone. The widow called her banker, a lifelong friend, and said, "I am amazed and bewildered by the manner in which the young people have squandered the money that my husband left them. It seems that my husband's death has made me see things in a different light. I want to be sure that I use my share of the estate wisely. Have you any suggestions?"

"Indeed I have," he told her. "I welcome the chance to discuss the matter with you."

When the banker saw her, he pointed out that she could expand the usefulness of her money by giving it to certain civic projects greatly needed in her community. He mentioned several of them to her, including a public library and an athletic field. He predicted that, in addition to aiding the town, she would broaden her own horizons of interest and satisfaction. She studied his suggestions carefully, launched several of the projects and followed them with intelligent participation. Later she told the banker, "I can never thank you enough for the help you gave me with my investments. When I see the boys and girls streaming out of the library with books under their arms, or watch the youngsters playing on the athletic field, I can hardly contain my happiness. The paths of personal service you have opened have revolutionized my life; there aren't enough hours in the day to do all the things I want to do. Life means more to me than it ever did before. To think, too, that I gave the money while I am still alive to enjoy the benefits! Certainly this is the way my husband would have wished it."

When Jesus said, "Give, and it shall be given unto you; good measure, pressed down, and shaken together, and running over," he was expressing not only a profound religious principle but also a realistic basis for personal happiness. "For with the same measure that ye mete withal it shall be measured to you again." To overcome our egocentricity is to defeat a powerful enemy of personal happiness. We can hope to find little more than a sampling of happiness until the vicious inward circle of self-interest is bent outward. Once the spiral is broken, we are free to become objective about ourselves and to engage in rewarding activities. We can establish a balanced relationship with others and with existence. When we turn away from our self-concern, our fears, our melancholy, our resentments and our regrets, replacing them with such healthy sentiments as love, hope, zest for life and a sincere interest in persons and incidents about us, we are adding *meaning* to our lives. We are making a fundamental adjustment toward getting a firm grip on happiness. Undoubtedly we shall encounter reverses and setbacks, but our persistence will produce growing evidence that we are headed in the right direction. In time the reward will justify the struggle, for even adversity will convert into capital gain.

s Dr. Fritz Kunkel pointed out, "It can be demonstrated that no power on earth can keep a subject on the dark side of life, who accepts life. The good will of people, the tractableness of one's family, success in one's work, and a tremendous growth in personal influence, productivity and happiness are the result of a positive attitude toward life." [5] Each of us can grow toward emotional maturity and therefore toward a greater degree of happiness, but not until we develop an unselfish devotion to that which fills our actions with meaning.

This leads to a consideration of the third facet of wholeness, that of *fulfillment*. In order to maintain happiness, we require not only unity and meaning, but also a sense of fruition. It is rewarding to feel that what we are is important to someone and what we do enriches the world in which we live. We get out of life not only what we take from it, but also what we put into it. Dr. Alfred Adler, in his individualistic approach to personality, declares that above all man wants to feel that he *counts*.[6] In each of us is the persistent urge to create something which is an outreach of ourselves. This rescues us from a depressing sense of uselessness. When we construct a bridge, clear a forest, build a business, fix a motor, fashion a chair, paint a picture, create a home, plant an idea in the plastic mind of a child, or grow prize-winning roses in the back yard, it adds to our sense of completion. This creative urge lies behind the desire for children; in the young life we bring into being, we give something precious to the world uniquely an extension of ourselves.

At times we cheat ourselves of such satisfaction because we misjudge the worth of our personal accomplishments. Because we assume that our achievements count for little, we become easily discouraged and a cloud of unhappiness envelops us. The beginning of a deeper happiness may come simply through a more realistic evaluation of our accon. plishments.

Call the roll of those who have meant most to the world and to their fellow men—not necessarily those who have basked in the limelight or caught the public fancy for a season—and we discover a list of earnest men and women who fell in love with their work and took a deep satisfaction in adding something constructive to the common good. A sincerely happy individual usually is one who has harnessed his abilities, mind and heart enthusiastically to an unselfish task. Once a visitor to Anton Lang's pottery shop in Germany expressed regret that Lang had retired from playing the Christus in the Oberammergau Passion Play. The aged workman replied, "I still feel I'm playing God if I shape things well."

Of late years, we have heard much about self-expression, usually with the connotation of throwing aside all restraints and of doing as one pleased. Defined in terms of personal freedom, it often degenerates into personal license. As a rebellion against authoritative discipline, unsoftened by insight or understanding, the impulse to "let oneself go" is easily comprehended, but this does not make it creditable. In reality, the fullest expression of self does not infer the liberty to express impulse without restraint; it comes close to meaning the exact opposite. As we forget ourselves in projecting something which is the extension of our heart, brain and skill, we most fully express ourselves—and most deeply gain a sense of fulfillment. Customarily, this calls for self-restraint, careful preparation and disciplined effort; in short, the denial of ourselves at many points. Dr. Gordon Allport has said that "self-expression requires the capacity to lose oneself in the pursuit of objectives *not* primarily referred to the self. Unless directed outward toward socialized and culturally compatible ends, unless absorbed in causes and goals that outshine self-seeking and vanity, any life seems dwarfed and immature." [7] When Jesus pointed out that the way to find one's life was to lose it, he was thinking not of repression but of fulfillment, not of denial but of self-expression. We have many selves within to express; happiness results when we fulfill our *best* selves and, without exception, that requires discipline, restraint and selectivity.

Some people consider self-expression as ruthless self-exploitation at the expense of other personalities. To express oneself, they assume, means to impose one's will, desires and pattern of action on others, without regard to their rights or sensibilities. But self-expression, rightly understood, does not mean the domination of others. The mature person takes delight in the expression of himself through his finest efforts, but simultaneously he freely allows others the same privilege. Nothing selfish, envious or arbitrary corrodes his spirit. Self-expression, as St. Paul wrote of love, "has good n.anners and does not pursue selfish advantage. It is not touchy. It does not compile statistics of evil or gloat over the wickedness of other people. On the contrary, it is glad with all good men when Truth prevails" (Phillips translation).

If our lives gain wholeness—integration, meaning and an adequate sense of fulfillment—the temporary unhappiness such as comes to all will not upset us. The surface waters may be disturbed, but underneath the surface the strong currents of happiness flow steadily. We find ways around our temporary setbacks. When we lose our job, we are confident that we can find a new one. When a dream shatters or a cause for which we have worked is defeated, we dream new dreams and find other worth-while causes. If our love is rebuffed, we find new expressions for our love. In fact, we strive to use all our crises for creative good. Each victory deepens our sense of unity, fulfillment and meaning. Thus we arrive; we gain maturity; we become complete—and completely happy—human beings.

CHAPTER II

The Habit of Happiness

HAPPINESS is closely associated with a mature, outgoing personality, as we have noted in the preceding chapter. A mature personality has acquired the habits and skills which can sustain happiness. We do not gather grapes from thorns, or figs from thistles; neither do we garner happiness until first we create the personal qualities which merit it. Integrity, loyalty, honesty, self-reliance, ingenuity, perseverance, cheerfulness, unselfishness, love, and the self-esteem that is at the heart of humility—these are among them. They do not emerge automatically; they are not the result of some lucky occurrence; they do not arrive *de novo*. They are acquired through years of training and effort, together with the disciplines and skills which become channels to express them.

A baby is born into the world as a bundle of unorganized, undirected energies. Everything must be done for him; he has no habits that can transmit his energies into purposeful action. It is impossible for him to focus his eyes, reach toward and grasp an object, place his hands together, or move forward by crawling. Later he masters these and other skills as he learns gradually to co-ordinate his movements and activities. As he grows older he gains more complex skills, such as running, jumping, writing and learning the multiplication table. These achievements are the result of habit patterns that he has established. Our mannerisms, the way we walk and talk, our methods of organization, our gestures, our ap-

34

proach to a person or a problem, and an infinite number of other responses all follow patterns determined by habit.

Through these various habits, the well-adjusted child harnesses his energies to actions which absorb the powers he pours into them. Daily he grows more mature in attitude, inner certainty and self-control as he gains greater knowledge and increasing skill. He acquires—and continues to acquire—habits which make him sufficient for the demands life makes on him. Each little victory gives added assurance. He attains skills that make him laugh at the memory of his early awkwardness in learning them, and that pay him rich dividends of enjoyment. He learns to marshal his resources and to apply them constructively to the problem at hand. He acquires objectivity concerning himself; when difficulties confront him, he does not flinch, or whine that fate has dealt him a foul blow. With the resources at his command, and sustained by the memory of former successes, he resolutely tackles each situation. Having overcome it, he has garnered valuable assurance that he is competent to deal with future difficulties, and has deepened the habit pattern which can lead to this happy result. And he has done something more. He has channeled his natural energies to constructive use, energies which otherwise would feed the fires of worry, fear, self-pity, resentment and an obsession with self.

The person who fails to develop a mature and outgoing pattern of behavior, who neglects to cultivate skills in a broad range of interests, falls into a subtle trap. When face to face with a new experience or a trying situation, he shrinks from it; the quickest way to eliminate conflict, he has learned, is to evade it. You cannot be defeated in a race you do not enter. Your rival cannot beat you in winning the heart of a girl if you do not court her. You cannot fail in a responsibility which you refuse to accept. The difficulty in such procedure, as is plain to be seen, is that it draws an individual more and more into the narrow confines of self, cuts off the possibility of growth and achievement, and thus thwarts the possibility of satisfaction and happiness. He cannot rely on past experiences or tested skills to carry him through; he has not acquired them, for he has shunned discipline and responsibility, and has feared the ridicule that might follow his awkward or unsuccessful efforts. Since he feels uncertain and insecure, he draws even more deeply into himself. In attempting to please himself, he has betrayed himself. In forming the selfish pattern of doing only what he has wanted to do when he felt like it, he has sabotaged his chances for happiness.

To make matters worse, because he has hoarded his energies and has not expended them in constructive activity, he now suffers from "nerves." He worries, has moods of depression, and wonders what life is all about or whether it is worth living. He is troubled by vague fears. He is dejected and unhappy. His inner life is much like a motor racing with the clutch out. It trembles and roars with power, but the power is not geared to the useful service for which the motor is intended. An engine is created to pull a load. So is the human machine; when we gear our energies wholeheartedly to a worth-while task, we are fulfilling a basic requirement for human happiness. Our personalities work with greater smoothness and efficiency. A sense of satisfaction lifts us and gives zest to living. If we choose to invest our energies in areas rich in helpfulness to our fellow men—in leading a boys' club, training a Scout troop, serving in a hospital, fighting for clean government, working in a church kitchen or conducting recreation on a playground—we are aligning ourselves with forces which can absorb our energies and grant deep personal satisfaction. It lies within our power to select such outlets and to form such habits.

One day I stopped the car at a traffic light and a police officer standing at the curb started toward me. I wondered what infringement of the law I had committed. When he asked if I were driving to a street several blocks ahead, I was greatly relieved by the nature of his question! As we rode along we struck up a conversation. I inquired how he liked his assignment in that area, which had a high rate of delinquency and crime. Enthusiastically he replied that he liked it fine. "There's always something going on," he explained in a rich Irish brogue. "You feel useful here. I used to be over near the Commissioner's home and there was nothing much to do but stand around all day. At the end of the month, it seemed almost a shame to draw my pay. But I did, all the same," he added, with a chuckle. "Finally I asked to be transferred over here and I'm glad I did. Something always is happening and a man feels useful." He described several of his experiences and some of them struck me as anything but pleasant; one or two made my skin prickle. Yet here was a man who overflowed with good cheer. "Why should it be so?" I asked myself. He was performing a useful service to the best of his ability. He was sincerely interested in people. He had formed outgoing habits of thought and action that left little energy for moroseness or unhealthy self-concern. As a result, he had a sense of satisfaction essential to sincere happiness.

When we concentrate our interests and energies on others rather than on ourselves, a quiet and peculiarly satisfying kind of happiness flows back in return. It is not necessary for our lives to be crammed with glamorous experiences and unusual opportunities, or to occupy the spotlight. If prominence and position pass us by, it does not mean that we must forswear joy and satisfaction. Happiness still can lodge with us, as the police officer's life attests. There are new interests to explore, fascinating activities to pursue and fresh services to render. An infinite number of skills challenge us, which may range from mountain climbing to baby sitting (it *is* a skill!), from flower arrangement to deep-sea fishing. The importance lies in the fact that we give our energies and interests to something sufficient to consume them. Whether the task is a scientific study, the preparation for a new job, the cultivation of an interest in another person, the performance of a distasteful task, the practice of a golf swing, or a drive to another city, it requires effort and discipline. Once we have trained ourselves to accept such demands as a matter of course and to tackle any assignment with enthusiasm, we have laid the groundwork for a healthy personality.

Habits are good or bad, depending on what they do for us. If they increase our total health and efficiency, they are good; if not, they are bad. We cultivate habits which induce and sustain happiness, or we form habits which invite unhappiness, "As a physician," wrote Dr. Richard C. Cabot of Harvard, "I have had the happiness of seeing work cure many persons who have suffered from trembling palsy of the soul which results from overmastering doubts, hesitations, vacillation and fear." [1] When we invest our lives we enrich them. A significant number of us need to understand ourselves more completely and to accept our lot more realistically; to channel our energies into outgoing habits and rewarding pursuits; to discipline our wills and to control our emotions; and, above all, to learn the inner truth of the Scriptural injunctions to "love thy neighbor as thyself" and that "it is more blessed to give than to receive."

Habits pertain to happiness in still larger terms. In addition to unselfish thoughts and outgoing skills, the *habitual attitudes* we assume are of utmost importance. We can form habits of hopefulness, patience, good cheer, love and fortitude toward whatever may happen to us, or we can allow ourselves to give way to bitterness, fear, resentment and self-pity. The choice is up to us; literally we can think ourselves happy, or we can think ourselves unhappy. The "set" of our emotional attitudes, determined through disciplined habit, governs the outcome.

A little girl once said to her mother at bedtime, "Mother, I've had such a happy time today."

"Really?" her mother smiled. "What made this day different from yesterday?"

The child pondered a moment. "Yesterday my thoughts pushed me around and today I pushed my thoughts around."

There is a world of wisdom in the child's observation. When we are morose and unhappy, often it is because we have not discovered the wise cherub's secret; we have let our thoughts push us around! When circumstances upset us, we permit ourselves to become panic-stricken and miserable instead of channeling our energies habitually into useful activities, utilizing them to turn our thoughts outward and away from ourselves. We grow sullen and envious of others because they achieve the successes for which we long. We allow the springs of love and tenderness to run dry. We set our hearts on certain goals and when they are not attained we fall into black and ugly moods. When we have mastered the habit of handling the bitter medicines of disappointment and hardship so that they do not rob us of well-being, happiness is within our reach. We will have discovered the faculty of extracting some pleasure from almost everything we experience. The chronically unhappy individual has not acquired this skill. Since all experiences are imperfect, he is constantly dissatisfied as they reach him. Since they are unsatisfactory today, they lend no enjoyment as they recede into the past. Since both the past and the present have failed to provide him with pleasure, he is cynical about receiving happiness in the future. Thus his whole existence—past, present and future—is doomed to unhappiness.

It need not be so. We all face reversals and setbacks; we encounter frustration and disappointment; we are forced to perform monotonous and distasteful tasks. But through the discipline of our attitudes we can find the satisfaction of accomplishment in almost any experience. An axiom in the cattle country states, "Life is not in holding a good hand, but in playing a poor hand well." The difference between happiness and unhappiness does not lie in the cards we receive but in the discrimination with which we play them.

We can form the habit of accepting life *in a spirit of gladness and gratitude.* In almost every experience, even when the outer husk seems rough and forbidding, a golden kernel lies within. But it never will enrich our lives unless a sense of appreciation gives us the faith to tear aside the husk. Like the miner who sifts the sands from his pan until only the rich nuggets remain, so we must sift the sands of existence in the pan of gratitude until the hidden nuggets of enduring worth are revealed. Most of us can take a lesson in gratitude from a little boy who was having a wonderful time playing with one roller skate. A man watching him remarked, "Sonny, you ought to have two skates."

The boy grinned up at him. "Sure, mister. I know I ought to have two skates. But you can have an awful good time on one skate if that's all you've got!"

To achieve real happiness it is essential to reflect the little lad's spirit. It aids immeasurably when we learn the habit of gratitude for what we have, even if it is not all that we may wish.

We start to receive and enjoy this kind of happiness right where we are. We need not move to another community, another apartment or another job. It is not necessary to wait until next month, or next season, or next year. The change begins when we cease to mourn for things we do not possess, and learn to appreciate the joys we have. Such blessings include a shy flower nestled almost unnoticed by the roadside; the smell of a log fire as we return from a long tramp through the woods; the wordless peace we feel as we gaze across the quiet acres at sunset; the touch of a baby's chubby hand on our cheek and the sight of his crooked three-toothed smile; the delicate tracery of ice-coated branches shining in the brittle sunlight; or the loyal twinkle in eyes you have learned to love. We are thankful for a quiet home, a few friends worthy of being loved and who love us in return, books that hearten and inspire, innocent pleasures that cause no sorrow and bring no pain, work to do and strength to do the work, good hopes and precious memories, a sincere religion empty of bigotry and full of kindness, a nation that in spite of her faults is still the greatest country in the world, where the widest opportunity and the sweetest freedom are to be found. Yet, unless we cultivate the habit of understanding and appreciation, we take our joys for granted and allow their blessings to escape us.

Another powerful ally in the attainment of happiness is *the attitude of love.* There are two basic securities which every well-adjusted personality must have. One is emotional security; lacking it, we cannot have durable happiness, no matter how favorable our position or circumstances may be. The second need is love. It is impossible to achieve emotional wholeness without it. In order to receive love, we must be mature enough to give it. If we find ourselves demanding love without being able to express it in return, we are emotionally ill.

This does not mean that we retain no interest in the fascinating creature called "ME." Self-respect, self-confidence and intelligent pride are stimulants to healthy achievement —when they are kept in proper balance. The Edinburgh weaver who prayed, "O Lord, give me a high opinion of myself," is not to be condemned as a conceited egotist; sincere self-esteem, scorning that which is shoddy and mean, can call out the best within us and can chain our loyalties to worthy ideals and high-minded action. It is only when we become egocentric that self-love proves harmful.

Healthy love protects us from such overbalance. Modern psychology reinforces the religious insight that, as we turn our thoughts and energies unselfishly from ourselves in an outreaching love, we gain emotional health and peace of mind. An interesting commentary lies in the fact that roughly three quarters of the patients in mental hospitals are persons who in childhood failed to learn to love. Not knowing how to receive or to express this basic emotion, they were forced to look for satisfaction within themselves, with the resulting growth of self-concern and the dominance of psychotic tendencies.

The child begins living as a self-centered individualist. Existence revolves around himself—his wants, his desires, his sensations. He demands that the world serve his whims and his needs. This self-assertiveness comes to a peak at age three or four. Then gradually, as his world expands beyond his family to playmates, school and teachers, he discovers that it pays to share some things with others. When he does, it brings approval and affection; when he refuses, he meets disapproval and animosity. He finds that it is rewarding to apportion to others the interest and love hitherto lavished on himself. True, he had learned this lesson first in relation to his parents, but the knowledge is strengthened through his growing contact with others. He becomes aware that as he gives he gets.

The further he proceeds in learning to express love, the more well-balanced he becomes. Emotional maturity demands that the individual receive more satisfaction in giving love than in receiving it. But such outgoing love does not travel a one-way street; the delightful aspect is that the more a person expresses unselfish love the more such love flows back to him. "We love to live; we live to love," wrote Lord

Acton. "It is the heart's food and nourishment, and the soul's highest bliss. Some other being must be blended with our own or else our existence is objectless."

Dr. Daniel A. Poling told of his mother, who, years ago, went as the bride of a young minister to do missionary work on the western frontier. Secretly she was resentful that her husband would take her into such hardships and danger. She was fearful of what lay ahead and pitied herself more than a little.

In the journey westward the wagon train came to a river swollen with floods. The caravan had to wait until the floods receded before it could cross. During the delay, a woman's tiny baby sickened and died. The bride, forgetting her fear and resentment, tried to comfort the bereaved mother. When at last they crossed the river to continue their journey, she traveled forward with a new spirit.

Years later Dr. Poling found her diary and read of this experience. She had written, "I found my peace when I held that sorrowing mother in my arms and when, in my own weakness and fear, I gave her all I had—my love!" In giving love we find happiness.

Finally, complete happiness rests on *a vital faith*. Such faith faces the enigmas of life and does not falter.

In the tender scene in the Upper Room, Jesus said to his disciples, "These things have I spoken unto you, that my joy might remain in you, and that your joy might be full. . . . In the world ye shall have tribulation; but be of good cheer; I have overcome the world." Soon he was to die in agony, taut against a cross. Yet his words were not uttered in derision or intended as mockery. He could speak them earnestly because his happiness rooted in something deeper than that which happened to him. No matter how viciously the winds of fate might rage, he believed that God still was in control of His world, and that the moorings would not slip. Even when facing a cross, he was certain of God's loving purpose for him and for all mankind.

It is difficult to find a radiant personality who has not sensed and appropriated a similar conviction as his own. One of the happiest and best-loved personalities of the American stage is Ethel Waters. When Miss Lucy Key Miller, newspaperwoman for the *Chicago Tribune,* visited Miss Waters in her dressing room, she found a charming and radiant person, proud of her success because of what it allowed her to do for others of her race. There was no arrogance in her pride, but a humble thankfulness. "I am grateful for what people see in me," she said. "I don't see it myself, and I never aspire to fame. I have just kept my feet on the ground, my head on a level plane. A quiet life would have suited me just as well. But I love the theater, and I have spent long and happy years in it."

The way toward acceptance and recognition during those years was not an easy road. She was acquainted at first hand with the struggles and hardships that any artist must meet. In addition, she encountered misunderstanding, intolerance and loneliness. At times it would have been easy to become cynical and embittered, yet she never lost her sense of inner joy. What held her steady in the dark hours was her deep and constant faith. "His eye is on the sparrow and on the turning of a leaf," she explained to the reporter; "I know He is watching me now." Her trust in God brought her serenity, taught her tolerance in a world of tensions and eased the heartbreak of defeat, loneliness and grief. Her faith is the foundation of a sincere happiness that her audiences sense and love.

Of all the attitudes which add a central core of steadiness to life, those inherent in a religious view of life are the most powerful. That the universe has meaning; that each individual is important in the ultimate scheme of things; that there are infinite forces on which the individual can draw to add amazingly to his personal power and magnify his individual significance; that God can turn even hardships and disaster into good; that the threatening gray wash of evil can advance only to pre-set limits before it is hurled back; that, although Truth, as James Russell Lowell observed, seems "forever on the scaffold," still "standeth God within the shadows, keeping watch above his own"; that, in spite of personal failures and grievous mistakes, we can find forgiveness and the power to start over; and that after earthly days are through, personal influence and life itself continue—such religious convictions inject meaning at every turn. In their light, life becomes a trust and therefore a challenge. When such faith dominates our attitudes, a strong sense of purpose permeates our wills and directs our actions. Our lives cohere around loyalties sufficient to pull them together into one piece. We become integrated, harmonized, one-directional; our energies fuse into concerted action. We discover that, whatever other characteristics God may have, fundamentally He is *loving*. We can turn to Him naturally and with trust as a child to a wise and understanding parent. Our entire basis for activity is reconstructed. "Love God," said St. Augustine with inspired insight, "and do as you please." If we love God enough, we strive to do as He would have us do; we yearn to please Him. We act freely, positively and with gladness, not from a sense of compulsion or fear. Faith, too, adds its strength and brightness, for if we love God we also can trust Him. We can move confidently in whatever direction life may dictate—forward, backward or seemingly no place at all —without resentment and without fear. Our spirits become flexible; we have faith that, wherever life may lead, the experience can be used for good; all things can serve our inner growth and wholeness. St. Paul expressed this conviction when he wrote, "We know that all things work together for good to them that love God, to them who are the called according to his purpose." Faith in the power and love of God thus liberates our energies for the happy business of *living*.

We need not concern ourselves with the uneasy thought that our religious convictions are an escape, built on unreality. Man's spiritual aspirations are as real as his hunger for bread. Recent psychiatric studies called "logotherapy"—the medical treatment of men's souls—have led to the conclusion that "we are born to believe," and that a considerable amount of psychosomatic illness can be traced to a repression of this fact. "Modern suppression of our need for religion," wrote Dr. M. Arthur Kline,[2] in explaining this view, "creates much of the frustration and tension in this atom-endangered world. It kills our chance for leading happy, purposeful lives." It is his belief that if men and women will recognize their need for a belief in God and in a meaning to life beyond their personal pleasures, they have enhanced greatly their ability to find peace of mind and happiness.

After mature consideration, it is easy to understand why this should be so. The deepest and most absorbing sense of meaning lies in answer to the outreach of our spirits toward God. Almost intuitively we recognize the power of religion to unify our lives around a core of supreme meaning. Professor C. S. Branden of Northwestern University made a study [3] in which over two thousand persons were asked why they were religious, after acknowledging that they were. Out of the sixty-five categories into which the answers were classed, the one most commonly expressed was that "religion gives meaning to life." Dr. J. A. Hadfield of England wrote, "Speaking as a student of psychotherapy, who, as such, has no concern with theology, I am convinced that the Christian religion is one of the most valuable and potent influences that we possess for producing that harmony and peace of mind and that confidence of soul which is needed to bring health and power to a large proportion of nervous patients." [4]

In our aspirations toward happiness, it is well to remember that we are *spiritual* beings—a truth which our modern day is likely to overlook. It is difficult to see how we can attain complete unity and the happiness which accompanies it when we ignore this fact. The spiritual hunger of humankind is as old as the race, and is no appendage or fantasy. The aspirations toward goodness, mercy, justice and truth are real, as genuinely a part of life as hunger, ambition and sex. "Holiness" in fact means *wholeness,* and wholeness is integral to any deep and lasting happiness, as we have discussed; invariably the happy person is a whole person. With all the charges which may be leveled at religion, it cannot be denied that religion has succeeded in giving a sense of meaning to countless lives.

In less strenuous centuries, it may have been possible to rally one's life around a lower stratum of moral values which largely ignored spiritual allegiance to a Supreme Being. But our age is one of upheaval, tensions, despairs and dangers. It is filled with conflict and chaos. It is next to impossible to withstand the shocks of such an age without the cushioning afforded by a sense of highest meaning, as the emotional breakdowns and overcrowded mental hospitals attest. Undoubtedly this fact also contributes to the spiritual hunger and the upsurge of religious interest that permeate our day. It is a healthy urge. In the universe is that which responds to personal allegiance, responds in such a way as to reward the seeker with stability and power. It adds a fourth dimension to our lives. Buried deep within, we possess something superior to circumstances.

CHAPTER III

Be Yourself!

UNIFIED living is impossible without the initial discovery and acceptance of oneself. In the process, we learn to guide ourselves by inner standards rather than attempt to live by external pressures and by what others expect. Thus we achieve happiness by finding personal independence in light of our true capacities.

It is not easy to come to terms with one's own individuality. Disruptive influences stand between the selves we are and the selves we desire to be. The human personality is complex and, like a carefully cut diamond, the self has many facets. We exhibit one side of self in the office or on the job, a second at home, another in the presence of superiors, and still another at a bridge party, on a fishing trip, or in the heat of athletic competition. Unless a sense of integration penetrates them all and binds them into one, the personality becomes a battleground of conflicting drives. When such inner discord exists, there can be no peace of mind or powerful, one-directional action.

Coupled with the multisidedness of personality, the influence others exert makes the problem of being oneself more difficult. We are strongly influenced by the desires and ambitions of those whom we love and admire, especially during the formative years of life. Such influence can be positive and creative, directing talents and ambitions toward worth-while goals, but also it can be stultifying and harmful to the devel-

48

opment of one's true self. Parents, for instance, can project their thwarted desires or unsatisfied ambitions into the minds of their children, although the abilities and temperaments of the children may be unfitted for success in these areas. A drygoods clerk, being frustrated in his burning desire to become a physician, transferred his ambition to his son. He assumed that the boy would study medicine and talked to him of little else; but the young man was not attracted to medicine and felt himself unfitted for the profession. Yet driven by a sense of loyalty he tried to shape himself into the mold of his father's ambition and finally broke under the strain. It was only after the young man learned to be himself and to be guided by his own ambitions that he discovered personal satisfaction and happiness.

To reach our highest potential we must begin *by accepting ourselves as we are* and not as someone expects or desires us to be. When we allow conscience or a sense of duty to drive us toward accepting the patterns laid down by someone else, or toward fashioning ourselves to artificial standards, we do so at the danger of grave unhappiness. Our own individual standard once discovered can provide an incentive that pulls our aptitudes and abilities together and harnesses them to achievement.

A second influence which leads to a warped personality is contemporary social pressure. Because the desire to be recognized and appreciated runs deep in human nature, one of the practical urges of man is to conform to the characteristic standards of the society of which he is a part. Therefore, he strives to mold himself into the accepted pattern of conduct and success, ignoring the fact that he may stifle and maim his native abilities in doing so. Suppressing the fundamental drives of his nature, he becomes restive, irritable and discontented. Ultimately he loses his zest for life. He questions its meaning. Unhappily he admits to himself that somehow he has missed the mark.

Illustrations of how social pressure can suppress the individual creative spirit are plentiful. A young man entered the corporation which his grandfather had founded, although his aptitudes and inclinations led to art rather than to business. The desires of his family and his social position made it difficult to do other than enter the firm. Now, after a quarter of a century of conscientious effort, he is an important executive of the corporation, but his mood is that of quiet desperation. Business success and expanded responsibility have not brought the satisfactions for which he hungers. Secretly he feels that the years have been wasted and that recognition in the business world cannot compensate for what he lost in failure to become an artist. Yet, when reminded that it is still possible for him to study art seriously, he advances numerous reasons why this is not feasible. The real reason is social pressure. He fears the disapproval of family, friends and associates.

Another man, tense and jittery, consulted his doctor. During the consultation he admitted that much of his trouble was caused by excessive drinking and gambling in order to keep up with his associates. "My nerves seem to be giving way," he said. The doctor advised him to curtail his gambling and give up drinking, or his condition would become serious indeed. "But, doctor, I can't!" the man replied. "If I quit now, my friends will think I'm a snob!" The visit ended on that note.

Young people especially are sensitive to social pressure. Rather than being the rebels the older generation pictures them, in reality they are amazing conformists. For example, they may consider their parents hopelessly old-fashioned, but they reflect their parents' opinions and prejudices in political views, religious convictions and social attitudes.

Then, too, there are the matters of dress and action. A new fad originates and every student on the high school or college campus must imitate it or feel apologetic; each dreads being considered "queer" for failing to conform. Take the blue-jean fad, for example. Not only must each young lady appear clad in blue jeans (which, by objective standards, are not the most flattering of feminine attire), but also one leg of the jeans must be rolled to the knee with the other folded half-way between knee and ankle! What dictated this arrangement is perplexing. Comfort might have called for both pant legs to be rolled to the knee; protection would require them not to be rolled at all. Now the craze is Bermuda shorts! In such uniformity, however, modern youth is not different from those who preceded them. Memory may take you back to the college campus on which no male was well dressed un-less bundled in a bulging racoon coat, and no girl was prop-erly attired unless buns padded her ears.

Social pressure leads both young people and adults to employ pretense. Because we want to stand high in the eyes of our fellows, we assume roles that we think will impress them. As children we played a game called "play like." We "played like" we were someone or something quite differ-ent from our true personalities. As we grow older, we are tempted to do much the same thing, although we may not recognize it. We pose as intellectuals, as men of important affairs, as women who are worn out by the social whirl. We strive to identify ourselves as martyrs of patience or paragons of virtue.

Usually the result of our pretenses is ridiculous; no one is fooled for long. Far more serious is the effect on one's own personality. The tension between the real and the assumed self can become intense. Conformity is one of the practical needs of mankind, but to try to force oneself into an unreal-istic mold invites unhappiness.

The struggle to become an artificial self often stems from feelings of inferiority. Basically, a sense of inferiority is an expression of insecurity. One fundamental need of healthy personality is security—we want to "belong." When we "belong," it is evident that we are desired and appreciated, both of which are essential to sound emotional adjustment. When we are rejected, it strips the sense of security from us, unless we are well-balanced personalities. Hurt and bewildered, we may become angry, blame others, give way to self-pity, or indulge in a mixture of these reactions. Lacking mature objectivity, we compare ourselves unfavorably with those who do "belong." We accuse ourselves of inadequacy. We flay ourselves with self-criticism and exaggerate our deficiencies. We magnify the poise and abilities of others. Feeling that we do not measure up to their competency or attractiveness, we assume that we are inferior. The result is a crushing sense of dejection and insecurity.

Inferiority feelings often originate in childhood. To feel supremely secure, a child must have love; if parents fail to supply love, the child's personality structure suffers. Most of the personality problems we face in adulthood as well as the behavior patterns with which we react to life originate in tender years. Suppose that a child is born into a family where he is not wanted. Perhaps the parents feel that the child's coming places an almost intolerable strain on the family's economic resources. Perhaps there is disharmony between the parents, or they resent the added responsibilities and the disruption of their pleasures. The child soon senses this rejection; long before he can put it into words, he feels that his parents do not love him. The result is almost overwhelming in its impact. His parents, and particularly his mother, represent the only security he knows. He *must* have something to which to cling. Therefore, he strives to buy their love. The coin he uses is that of "being good," which means submissiveness, meekness and self-debasement. In striving never to incur their displeasure he stifles normal impulses of aggression and self-expression. To make matters worse, try as he will to live up to the impossible standard which he has set for himself, he makes mistakes and brings on himself the wrath of his parents. With something akin to panic, he strains even harder to be "good"; his sense of insecurity deepens, and with it his feelings of inferiority. So he comes to consider himself less clever, less talented and less efficient than those about him. The distorted relationship based not on true love but on fear has resulted in an unhealthy personality pattern.

The victim of deep-seated inferiority feelings tries to escape from them in a number of ways. One method is through fantasy, or daydreaming. He compensates for his real or fancied inabilities and weaknesses by projecting himself into a land of make-believe in which his awkwardness and inefficiencies vanish. He envisions himself as clever, successful and adored. Daydreaming has its normal function, but when it becomes abnormal so that the imagined world is as real as the objective world, or when it is difficult to perceive where fact leaves off and fantasy begins, the individual has gravely penalized his chances of dealing constructively with himself.

Others, feeling inferior and insecure, turn in a different direction. They exaggerate their incompetency. They tell themselves they cannot possibly succeed and therefore it is useless to try. They eliminate the possibility of defeat or failure by refusing to make an effort. A student convinces himself, "My I.Q. is lower than that of the others in my class. That's why I'm at the bottom of the ratings." Or a girl reasons, "I don't have the charm or ability that other girls possess. What's the use of trying?" Their argument relieves them of all personal responsibility. A "defeatist" attitude, a lack of self-confidence and a refusal to apply the abilities they possess represent the basic difficulty. A stubborn sense of inferiority can expand such feelings to a flight from reality through imagined illness or neurotic behavior.

A common response to a sense of inferiority is to compensate for it through aggressive action. In the effort to hide a torturing sense of deficiency, the individual blusters and swaggers, becomes boastful and domineering. The man small in stature assumes a cocky attitude and carries an emotional chip on his shoulder. The self-conscious woman talks effusively, drives herself hard to prove herself capable and is savagely critical of others' shortcomings. The businessman, haunted by a sense of failure, exaggerates his superiority. He must win at all costs. The overaggressive action is both a mask to cover the inner feelings and an attempt to gain revenge on other persons whose only fault is to seem more sufficient than the troubled individual.

Another difficulty which many encounter in the struggle to be themselves is a rigid sense of perfectionism. They demand of themselves and others an impossible standard of conduct and action. Perfectionism becomes an armor with which they seek to shield themselves from adverse criticism and disfavor. They attempt to find satisfaction in feelings of personal superiority.

This explains why a woman will appear in public always dressed in the height of fashion, horror-struck at the thought of being seen in something on which the latest mode may frown. This reveals why a man strives never to make a mistake in grammar, or accomplishes his work with exactness in an infinite number of small details. Perfectionism prevents a woman who has studied music from singing in a group where someone of superior attainments may be present, or a man from taking a more responsible position because of the risk of failure. Perfectionism is the reason some women slave to keep the house in perfect detail at all times and to vent their anger on anyone in the household unfortunate enough to disrupt it. A husband made bold to bring two friends home one afternoon. He left them in the living room briefly and on his return one of them was gone. "Where is Jim?" he asked. The friend explained that Jim had stepped into the bathroom to remove a tiny cinder from his eye. "I hope he doesn't drop it on the floor," the host said anxiously, "or I'll catch it from my wife!"

The demand for perfectionism lies behind many of the patterns which characterize our industrial, professional and social life. The businessman *must* stand first in his field; dog-eat-dog competition is the result. The professional man *must* be well thought of; he seizes every opportunity to place himself above his fellows. Socially, the perfectionist *must* have a home bigger than his neighbors, a salary greater than his associates, a car more sleek and powerful than those of his friends; he must live in a community, a state and a nation that is "the best in the world." He is not noted for his understanding and appreciation of the good qualities in other cultures, other races and other lives. He is governed by what others think; at all costs he must maintain the appearance of superiority and perfection in the eyes of those about him. Moreover, when he indulges in kindness or performs a charity, he expects the recipients to be grateful. A character in a Broadway play was described as a man who "did what he considered to be his duty toward his family, his community and his God, and he expected all three to appreciate it." [1] The perfectionist is never satisfied with himself until he receives the applause of others.

This unswerving insistence on perfection actually is the result of a humiliating sense of inferiority. At all costs he must hide it from the view of his fellows, so he battles grimly for superiority. He must have it to bolster his ego, yet all the while he is unhappy and fearful that others will penetrate his pretense. This spirit carries over into every area of his life, including his expression of religion.

Recall the unwanted child who tried to buy his parents' love by "being good." In due time he becomes conscious of other forces beyond his parents in his little world. Soon he is aware of God and, since every child first conceives of God in the image of his parents, God becomes for him an inscrutable Power whom he must propitiate at all costs. He feels forced to buy God's favor by "being good," as he has attempted to placate his parents; otherwise he fears that he will fall from God's favor and be punished. Worse still, he will lose the spiritual security which God represents. His relationship to God becomes that of anxious fear, not the "fear" of God as used in the Scriptures, which means a loving reverence of the Divine. As with his parents, he strives never to make a mistake or to break the immutable laws which he feels that God has ordained. If he does, he is terrified by the punishment which he is certain God will inflict on him. As he grows into manhood, he strives to repress the drives and instinctual forces surging within him which seem to drive him counter to the stern "thou shalt nots" which the Eternal Judge has decreed. When in spite of himself he does something denied by his inflexible moral code, a sense of guilt and remorse sweeps over him. Attempting to right the situation, he strives all the harder not to make additional mistakes and thus to run further risk of falling from God's good graces. God, he feels, has small tolerance for human weakness.

The relation is based not on the creative force of love, but on hate, and becomes impossible. Being human, he can never reach perfection, no matter how hard he tries, so his sense of guilt and frustration continues to mount until in time the tension becomes unbearable. It is as if he were living in a room with an overbearing landlord above and a group of fiendish tormentors dwelling below. The landlord pounds on the floor and the sadistic neighbors bang on the radiator pipes until the unfortunate tenant is driven to distraction.

The church must assume its share of the blame for this rigid moral perfectionism and the resulting misconception of God. It cannot be denied that in the minds of many the church is associated with repression and self-denial. This is due in no small part to the influence of nineteenth-century puritanism and its unyielding moral code. Puritanism, to be sure, had many fine qualities and produced exceptional fruits. In its richest expression it gave birth to moral power and creativity. However, it degenerated into a negative suppression of the natural impulses and a jaundiced view of human happiness. The "desires of the flesh," being associated with original sin, were ruthlessly repressed. Almost the only satisfaction of desire deemed acceptable was the satisfaction derived from denying desire. To enjoy life fully, to laugh and be happy, to eat with zest, or to play with abandon were held suspect. If these were examined closely, it was thought, they would reveal the hidden hallmark of the devil.

Great numbers of people have dissociated themselves from the church, considering it an instrument of unrealistic and antiquated authoritarianism, and "self-expression" has become a byword in modern life. Yet one who deals with the emotional problems of individuals is amazed constantly at the persistent influence of unhealthy puritanism on the moral convictions of the confused people who talk with him. They demand of themselves a rigid perfectionism impossible to attain and which leads to frustration, self-punishment and unhappiness.

A woman believes that she never should feel resentment against her mother because it is not dutiful or "right." The thought of such resentment horrifies her, but her inner life is filled with a hostility that curdles her emotions and wrecks her health. A man holds himself to a superlative moral code, but is heartily disliked because he constantly sits in judgment on others' actions, assumes a holier-than-thou attitude and is uncharitable in his outspoken criticism. A woman is convinced that it is a sin to get angry and turns a bland countenance to every exasperating situation, but her life is harried by neurotic symptoms for which she cannot account or understand. A young man, under the bondage of his childhood training that there is something nasty about sex, and mindful of the Scriptural injunction that "every one who looks at a woman lustfully has already committed adultery with her in his heart," is ashamed of the impulses which well up within him in spite of his efforts to repress them. He resolves to control his thoughts more rigidly, but his desperate efforts to do so lead to incongruous results. He may have a compulsion to work feverishly with no letup; he is deeply anxious about things of little consequence; he experiences increasing difficulty in concentrating; he finds it hard to fall asleep at night and, when he does, violent dreams disturb his slumber. At last, often unexpectedly, an emotional or moral breakdown occurs.

The path leading out of this maze of pretense and disruptive tensions is that of healthy self-acceptance. This state of mind requires that we accept individual limitations and imperfections and refuse to worry about them. We try to better ourselves, to be sure, but we come to the realization that no one is perfect, nor is a human being expected to be. Human nature is composed of a mixture of good and evil, as through the centuries the masters of literature, poetry and theology have pointed out, to be joined more lately by the psychologists. St. Paul's classic words describe the struggle: "For the good that I would I do not: but the evil which I would not, that I do. . . . O wretched man that I am! who shall deliver me from the body of this death?" Through all existence, bad intertwines with good, imperfection with perfection, wrong with right. Healthy-mindedness requires that we realize and accept the fact of imperfection in our moral make-up; then this realization can help us turn even our imperfections to creative use.

When we lay aside the impossible burden of being perfect, with its attendant sense of remorse and guilt, we come to the knowledge that God does not resemble a loveless human parent. We need not strive to buy His favor since God does not love us because we are good, make no mistakes and cause Him no trouble. God loves us because He is God; He cannot help loving us, any more than a true parent can help loving his stubborn, foolish, naughty or rebellious child. On our part, we put aside pretense, insecurity and false pride. Sustained and inspired by a love that will not let go of us, no matter what the circumstances, we strive to live up to the Divine trust imposed in us and to do the best with what has been given. We are sorry for our failures, but not demoralized by them. When we stumble, we pick ourselves up and make a fresh start. We are relieved of the necessity of making a "good impression" either on God or on our fellow men. This in itself is a burden lifted, for, as William James has pointed out, to give up pretense can bring as blessed a relief as having a pretension gratified. We are free to be *ourselves* and the way is open for healthy self-acceptance.

We can lay aside the unhappy burden of acting a part. We resolve to do our best with what we have, to stand or fall by the product of our own mind, heart and hands. "No man," said Samuel Johnson, "was ever great by imitation." We realize that a mature personality does not shift the cause of defeat or failure to someone else or to something outside himself. When a competent golfer develops a streak of wildness, he does not blame it on his fellow players or on the layout of the course. To improve his game, he looks to himself. "What is the matter with me?" he asks himself. "What

am I doing incorrectly?" Honesty and sportsmanship demand that he refuse to alibi and that he accept personal responsibility for the bad shots as well as for the good. A
similar obligation confronts us in the game of life. Even when
disaster overtakes us, we alone select the response to that
which happens to us. In this sense, the real tragedy or triumph is never due to outside forces; it lies within.

> The fault, dear Brutus, is not in our stars,
> But in ourselves . . .

In the process of accepting ourselves, it is essential to look
at ourselves realistically, noting both our strengths and our
weaknesses, and to evaluate ourselves as we really are. Since
many people go through life as complete strangers to themselves, how can they discover the unity of personality which
is the foundation for lasting happiness? "A sincere man," declared Carl Gustav Jung, "knows that even his bitterest opponent, or any number of them, does not by any means equal
his worst adversary. That is, his other self, who hides within
his breast." [2]

Such self-acceptance means resignation, but not resignation in an indolent or passive sense. It is dynamic and creative. In spirit, we say to ourselves, "Now I have found out
what I have to work with. I wish it were more, but it is the
best I have. Let's see what I can accomplish with what's
available!" The ground is cleared for creative endeavor. In
his essay, "Self-Reliance," Ralph Waldo Emerson wrote:
"There is a time in every man's education when he arrives at
the conviction that envy is ignorance; that imitation is sui-
cide; that he must take himself for better, for worse, as his
portion; that though the wide universe is full of good, no
kernel of nourishing corn can come to him but through his
toil bestowed on that plot of ground which is given to him
to till." When that time arrives in the process of individual

growth, our feet are planted on the highway leading to personal satisfaction and peace.

Such self-acceptance is realistic, humble and self-respectful. It gives power to turn even deficiencies into stimuli toward achievement. An impressive example lies in the life of Henry Fawcett, a brilliant student at Cambridge University. On a hunting trip shortly after he graduated, he was wounded by gunshot and completely lost his eyesight. During convalescence, he was in a turmoil of agony. He bitterly resented his blindness and the seeming end to his usefulness. Although he was only twenty-five years of age, his friends urged him to resign himself to his fate. Then a letter arrived from a former instructor that brought light into his rebellious darkness. The letter read in part, "It must be our own fault if such things are without their alleviation. Give up your mind to meet the evil in the worst form it can assume. It will lose half its terrors if regarded steadfastly in the face." [3]

The letter stirred a vigorous response in Henry Fawcett. He resolved to accept his limitations and to face them constructively. He began to follow a systematic program of work and study which the instructor had outlined for him. Some years later he became a professor of economics at Cambridge. Eventually he was the postmaster general of England and a member of the British cabinet.

It is possible to say that Henry Fawcett attained his success in spite of his handicap, but that is only part of the truth. The incentive behind his eminent success was that he accepted himself and his handicap, finding in such resignation a spur which called forth his finest abilities. His is not an isolated incident. The human personality, the unified self, is not something with which we are born; it is achieved. Often the stimulus of a defeat awakens power to hasten unity and achievement. In fact, after observing humanity in its strivings for inner satisfaction, one becomes convinced that whatever hinders a man, if it does not defeat him, aids him in his upward climb.

Although not everyone has to face as staggering a handicap as Henry Fawcett, or is able to achieve such an amazingly successful response, a personally satisfying compensation is almost always possible, once we have made the initial act of thorough self-acceptance.

A plain-featured young woman, cherishing recognition and affection, realized that she never would attract others by physical beauty. She accepted the fact and determined that, although she could not be the most beautiful girl in her set, she could be the most friendly and helpful. Her sincere spirit of service and outgoing friendliness won for her the affection and popularity she desired.

A boy loved music and studied the organ, but had to face the bitter realization that he did not possess the talent to become an exceptional organist. He resigned himself realistically to the situation, evaluated his aptitudes and inclinations, and entered a technical college to study electronics. His education was interrupted by the war, but after being detached from the service he completed his degree, won a commission in the navy and now is happily engaged in naval electronic experiments.

A girl, after the death of both parents, found herself suddenly transplanted from the country to the crowded city and into a difficult adjustment in the large family with whom she lived. She became shy, discouraged and morose. One day a kindly working woman, noting her seated dejectedly on a step, stopped to pat her on the head and say, "Life ain't all you want, but it's all you got. So stick a daisy in your hat and be happy." Something in the words and the kindly action stirred the girl's spirit and drove back her hopelessness. The next day she found a job at the only kind of work she knew, laboring with her hands. But it was the beginning of a new day which led ultimately to the establishment of a successful business and to the discovery of personal happiness.[4]

In achieving successful adjustment, there is a step beyond self-acceptance—the substitution of positive for negative attitudes. The plain young woman, the thwarted organist, the dejected girl each refused to assume a defeatist attitude and presented an aggressive, confident spirit to their difficulties. Multitudes live unhappy and miserable lives because they have failed to do likewise. The way to self-acceptance and personal satisfaction often lies simply in a shift of attitude. When an individual, filled with self-concern and despair, directs his attention outward with a positive spirit of trust and enthusiasm, he is in the process of becoming a more happily integrated personality.

Our lives are largely the sum total of the attitudes we take and the thoughts we think. The mental images we cherish, the habitual disposition with which we meet experiences and people, the thoughts we hold, and the emotions which color our actions determine fundamentally the kind of persons we are. There are two approaches possible to almost every situation. One is from the negative point of view, the other is from the positive; we ourselves determine which attitude we take. A propensity to resentment, fear and distrust is an almost insurmountable barrier in the path to self-acceptance, while a realistic but confident submission to oneself is healthy and creative. Elbert Hubbard wrote, "Picture in your mind the able, earnest, useful person you desire to be, and the thought that you hold is hourly transforming you into the particular individual you admire." The Book of Proverbs declares, "For as [a man] thinketh in his heart, so is he." The Apostle Paul adds, "Be ye transformed by the renewing of your mind."

"Transformed," meaning to be revitalized, turned around, re-formed, is not too strong a word. The attitudes we assume dictate our responses to the shifting experiences of life, and thus shape our destiny. When we face the world with rancor, with what vindictiveness it stares back at us! When we look at it with an expansive, friendly and faith-filled spirit, how co-operative and creative it can become! Perplexities and tragedies do tangle life, but when accepted with trust and assurance they become simply obstacles placed in the testing ground of experience to toughen our moral fiber and to strengthen character. We can allow bitter, resentful, envious thoughts to rule our minds, or we can center our attention on what is kind, just, pure, lovely and of good report. The final choice is ours. Remember that when we select the lower rather than the higher, *the choice is not forced on us.*

Successful personal adjustment also includes the realization of the individual's unique contribution to the welfare of the world. No two personalities are alike. Each of us, no matter how unimportant we may feel, or how humble a position we may occupy, has his own singular worth. It is ours, and ours alone, to give to humanity that which lies within our personalities; therefore, we need not be envious of another's talents or place in society. We are under no obligation to struggle to emulate him, nor have we cause to belittle his accomplishments. Even a humble life can bear a great message. A battered canteen can carry life-giving water. Although we are not fashioned as giant dynamos, we still can hum merrily with help and good cheer. We may not be sleek and powerful limousines, but a jeep can go places and accomplish things impossible to a limousine. Every man has reason to thank God that he is *himself* and different from other men, not in the sense of being superior, but of being distinctive. It is common sense and makes for emotional well-being to accept our individuality gratefully and to use it constructively.

There is an attractiveness in individuality, as nature reveals. What if the pine tree should strive to resemble the oak, and the poplar should eat its heart out to blaze with the glory of an autumn maple? What if the crow should attempt to coo like a dove, and the thrush to flash with the fire of a cardinal? But each segment of nature, even the earthworm, has its own usefulness or beauty to release in the world. Each performs its highest function by being itself.

> The mountain and the squirrel
> Had a quarrel,
> And the former called the latter "Little Prig";
> Bun replied,
> "You are doubtless very big;
> But all sorts of things and weather
> Must be taken in together
> To make up a year
> And a sphere.
> And I think it no disgrace
> To occupy my place.
> If I'm not so large as you,
> You are not so small as I,
> And not half so spry.
> I'll not deny you make
> A very pretty squirrel track;
> Talents differ; all is well and wisely put;
> If I cannot carry forests on my back,
> Neither can you crack a nut."

In the realm of personality, the principle is the same; there is attractiveness in individuality. Each one of us, no matter how humble our station in life, has worth and dignity in the eyes of God. It is said that Sir Michael Costa, the nineteenth-century Italian conductor and composer in England, once stopped the orchestra in the rehearsal of a resounding passage to inquire, "Where is the piccolo?" Perhaps the piccolo player had become careless, supposing that his contribution was of no importance. To the conductor the piccolo was needed to create the perfect harmony he desired. We may feel that our instruments of personality are insignificant and will not be missed. But in the orchestration of life, each of us has a part to play and the obligation to play it well. This we do by accepting ourselves as we are and by making the best of what we have.

CHAPTER IV

Faith and Happiness

IN ADDITION to accepting ourselves as we are, another essential step toward the achievement of happiness is the application of faith to the practical problems of every day. At once the question arises, what is faith? "One cannot pluck it out of thin air," a sincere critic observes. "I have tried to apply faith to my personal problems, but it doesn't work; either it's powerless or there must be something about it that I don't understand."

Such an honest statement deserves earnest consideration—and a straightforward answer. There is nothing occult about faith, a mystical magic which only the initiated can wield. Nor is it a theological phenomenon with sanctity for the chosen few. Faith, when rightly understood, is as practical as meat and potatoes and, at the same time, contains enough spiritual dynamite to explode old habits of thought and action—enough to transform our lives. Faith is not even something that we must acquire, but it is a faculty that each of us *has*, as the pages ahead will explain.

Today it is easy to deny the practicality—or even the possibility—of faith, and to fall into a cynical mood which corrodes every area of existence it touches. It is the "Oh yeah?" mood; the attitude of "What do I get out of it?" It is the mood of the flippant wisecrack, which often covers a quavering fear. Lawrence of Arabia, the gifted man who gained prominence in the era following World War I, declared that doubt is modern man's crown of thorns. It is due in part to the fact that many of the noble assurances which upheld our grandparents have shriveled for us and lost their authority. The landmarks which to them were sharp and clear have dimmed for us in the fog of uncertainty. The anchors of faith have slipped their moral moorings. In the channel of life someone seems to have removed the buoys that marked the shallow water and dangerous reefs, and we navigate today with extreme difficulty. This is true in the realm of business, politics and religion, as well as in personal and public morals. In every area of existence where the human mind plays a part, we feel the chill touch of doubt and cynicism.

In part this is due to a sense of nervous exhaustion, as well as to shifting moral landmarks. Our nerves are frayed, our strength drained and our wills tired. Our generation has tried to live a maximum life on a minimum faith and the inevitable consequences now result. Small wonder that men go to pieces under the strain. "No civilization," said Woodrow Wilson, "can long survive the demise of its religious faith." Both in our personal experience and in the world at large, so many dreams have been broken, so many hopes crushed, and so many desires mutilated that we wonder if aspirations ever reach fruition or if hopes ever become a reality.

We read in the Scriptures, "This is the victory that overcometh the world, even our faith," and we admit that in a far-off courageous day faith did add power and certainty to individual lives. But we hear the words wistfully or with stoicism, for such certitudes seem like the echoes of a poignant song heard long ago. Secretly we wish that we might have a faith sufficient to buttress us against the hardships and pitfalls of existence. We recognize that without it something radiant and precious eludes us, for we sense that without trust in something, there can be no enduring happiness or oneness of spirit. Without belief, life becomes a hollow and disappointing affair.

Even as we make a tremulous bid for faith, a brutal experience may throw us back into a mood of bitterness and distrust. A friend of mine was having lunch with an acquaintance, an attorney, who leaned forward and asked in anguished voice, "How can I have faith?" Then he told this story.

Before the state elections, he had been approached by a candidate, who was running for an important office, with the request to become the candidate's campaign manager. If the candidate were successful, he would see that the attorney received an office in the municipal government which eventually would lead to a judgeship. To accept the responsibility as campaign manager meant that he must take a leave of absence from his law firm. With the consent of his two partners, he decided to do so.

He conducted the campaign with such ability and imagination that his candidate was elected. He waited for his promised appointment, but it was not forthcoming. After two months, he met the candidate and asked when he was to receive the new office. Bluntly the politician told him that he was under political pressure that he had not foreseen; he considered his agreement as a campaign promise, and had no intention of fulfilling it. Angry words followed which destroyed the friendship of a lifetime.

Stunned by such treatment, the attorney consoled himself with the thought of his law practice. When he informed his partners that he was ready to return, they told him that, although he was free to resume his place in the firm, he would have to take a smaller percentage of the earnings than he formerly had commanded. They pointed out that his knowledge of law and his capacity for research were valuable to the firm, but he failed to bring in a proportionate share of clients. One of the partners, having accepted responsibility in Washington, D.C., found that he needed a greater share of the profits to meet added expenses; the other had attained a social status which required the larger income he had received in the absence of the third partner. It was simply a matter of arithmetic, they pointed out. It was after this conference that, choked with emotion, he had asked my friend, "How can I have faith?"

Such distressing circumstances give birth to practical atheism. There are few philosophic atheists in our generation, men and women who after serious soul-searching and intellectual struggle are led to the denial of God. But there are many who, wounded and confused by the brutalities of life, turn cynical and distrustful. In the light of hard facts, faith seems to them unrealistic and impractical. They feel that only weaklings, the unintelligent, and those who have not "lived" can retain faith.

Part of the difficulty is due to confusion as to the nature of faith. We assume that it means to believe a creed, dogma or religious formula which we cannot accept. The reason we refuse may be that we have not troubled to study it carefully or to discover the inner vitality which gave birth to that particular creed, dogma or formula, and which has sustained it through the years. Howbeit, it has no meaning for us and, thinking that faith demands its acceptance, we say that we have no faith and go our heedless or wistful way.

The discerning skeptic notes, also, that there are those who practice faith in the nature of a political campaign. They attempt to strike a bargain with God. In effect they say, "God, we will work for you as long as we get what we expect in return. If we fail to receive adequate compensation, the contract is off. We then will swing our influence and our votes to the other side. That candidate seems to have a way of rewarding those who work for him!" They expect value received—and a trifle more. They resemble Jacob who prayed at Bethel: "If God will be with me, and will keep me in this way that I go, and will give me bread to eat, and raiment to put on, so that I come again to my father's house in peace; then shall the Lord be my god . . . and of all that thou shalt give me I will surely give the tenth unto thee." But if not, evidently the contract would be null and void. It was not a bad bargain! But the self-respecting seeker turns his back on such practice and assumes that it is impossible for him to have faith.

Also, he may reject faith because he thinks that it means credulity. He assumes that faith is what the little boy said it was, "believing something that ain't so." In his search for faith, the modern man refuses to outrage his sensibilities by accepting something so naïve and unrealistic that it demands gullibility. He lives in a hardheaded universe where laws govern both the conduct of the spheres and the human personality. He resolves to trust reason and not to profane it by believing something that isn't so, no matter how much such a featherbed of credulity might protect him from the jolts of life.

A humorous passage in *Through the Looking Glass* deals with faith in this sense. Alice declares that there are some things in which she cannot force herself to believe. The Queen replies in pitying tones, "Can't you? Try again. Draw a deep breath and close your eyes." Some think that this is a fairly accurate description of faith—a matter of closing one's eyes, drawing a deep breath and becoming gullible. In loyalty to reason and intellect, they are convinced that they cannot have faith.

Such persons are mistaken as to the nature of faith, for faith is something far different from credulity. Credulity swallows without testing; true faith demands to know where the medicine comes from and what good it may be expected to accomplish. In the pursuit and discovery of truth, in whatever area of attainment, one proceeds from the known to the unknown. The method of doing so involves the use of hypothesis or supposition. Such hypotheses are not facts, but are considered opinions on which one ventures in the pursuit of facts. One attempts to verify hypotheses by testing them in relation to established facts. This is the method of the scientist, the philosopher and, at his best, the religious man. Both the art of living and the attainments of science depend on forming sufficient and satisfying conclusions from insufficient premises.

During a convention of the nation's leading scientists, I had an extended conversation with one of them. He talked about some of the marvelous achievements of science during the last quarter of a century. He was especially interested in the extraction of minerals and other resources from the sea and spoke with such enthusiasm that I remarked, "You seem to sense amazing possibilities in the study of oceanography."

He smiled and answered earnestly, "Yes, but what we have discovered thus far is nothing compared to what we are going to develop during the next ten years."

"How do you know that?" I asked.

"I *don't* know it as an established fact," he admitted, "but I believe it beyond all doubt."

In the field of science, it seems evident that men walk not by sight but by insight, and are led to fact through faith. Indeed, the eminent physicist, Max Planck, states that over the portal to the temple of science these words should be inscribed: *Ye must have faith.* The scientist must thrust beyond the known into the unknown through daring hypothesis if he is to push back the horizons of factual knowledge and add to scientific advance. In this sense, all progress rests on faith—faith in the reality of truth, faith in the human mind to discover truth, and faith that things have a meaning. The

scientist's term for such conviction is "hypothesis," while the
religious man calls it "faith." In either case, it is "reason
grown courageous."

> There is no unbelief;
> Whoever plants a seed beneath the sod
> And waits to see it push away the clod,
>   He trusts in God.

> Whoever says when clouds are in the sky,
> "Be patient, heart; light breaketh by and by,"
>   Trusts the most High.

>   . . .

> Whoever says, "Tomorrow," "the unknown,"
> "The future," trusts that Power alone
>   He dares disown.

>   . . .

> There is no unbelief;
> For thus by day and night unconsciously
> The heart lives by the faith the lips deny.
>   God knoweth why! [1]

Consider how faith motivates the scientist in his quest for
new knowledge. Charles Kettering invented the self-starter
for the automobile. After he had proved that the self-starter
worked, he addressed a group of scientists at a meeting of
the American Institute of Electrical Engineers and explained
the principles governing the self-starter. When he had finished his speech, one of the men present arose and said, "Mr.
Kettering, no wonder you made the self-starter work; you
have profaned every law of electrical engineering!"

Later, in discussing this incident, the inventor said that he
had not profaned a single fundamental principle of electrical
engineering. What he had done was to form a hypothesis
which put principles together in fresh relationships. Then he
tested his hypothesis and it worked. Note that the applica-

tion of electrical laws in a new approach was first of all an act of faith on the inventor's part.

Lord Kelvin, the prolific inventor (the Kelvinator takes its name from him), once declared that he never reasoned his way to any of his discoveries. He explained that he brooded over the facts relevant to his problem and suddenly, in a great moment, "came an inward look, a life-and-death leap into the unknown." He felt that the solution lay there, and so it did. Faith led to a hypothesis and the hypothesis to a discovery of fact.

That which is accepted on "faith" should not contradict any proven fact, any more than the scientist's hypothesis can do so. In either case, whether hypothesis or faith, it should be the springboard which launches the adventurous spirit into the unknown in the quest of new knowledge. Faith is as vital to the religious outreach of life as hypothesis is to the scientist in the pursuit of factual knowledge about the mysterious universe which surrounds him. Whether in the field of science, business, sociology, romance or religion, faith is a working hypothesis. It is the motivating force that makes decision and action possible. It is an adventure of the spirit; it ends not with argument but in action. Dean William R. Inge included such conviction when he defined faith as "the resolution to stand or fall by the noblest hypothesis." Donald Hankey expressed it even more pungently, "Faith is betting your life that there is a God."

The most famous definition of faith appears at the opening of the eleventh chapter of the Book of Hebrews, "Now faith is the substance of things hoped for, the evidence of things not seen." It can be paraphrased to read, "Faith is the assurance of things hoped for, the testing of things not seen." The heroes named in the roll call of this Westminster Abbey of faith did exactly that. Certain that the things for which they hoped could become a reality, they put the assurance to the test. Convinced that God had a purpose for their lives and that His presence would sustain them in the time of trial, they dared to venture out on that conviction, testing it as a working hypothesis. They discovered that it worked! They "through faith subdued kingdoms, wrought righteousness, obtained promises, stopped the mouths of lions, quenched the violence of fire, escaped the edge of the sword, out of weakness were made strong, waxed valiant in fight, turned to flight the armies of the aliens." Faith to them was neither credulous nor academic; faith was tested power.

But faith cannot become "tested power" for us until we venture on it in the practical affairs of life. Psychologists point out that both belief and doubt are living attitudes, and involve *conduct*. We express belief or doubt by living accordingly. We can live "as if" various fundamentals were true or untrue. We can live "as if" the universe were blind, mechanistic and unheeding, or that a creative, personal, loving Force moves through it—and us. We can live "as if" ruthlessness, brutality and force were the ultimate powers; Stalin held this concept, as have others. We can live "as if" the universe were centered in us, our desires, our wishes, our will. Or we can live "as if" goodness will triumph over evil and hope transcend despair. We can approach life "as if" the true values lie not in the seen and transient but in the unseen and eternal.

The conviction on which we determine to act shapes our conduct. We can live "as if" our doubts were true and our hopes traitors; we can refuse to believe in beauty in whatever form we find it; we can deny that there are decent, kindly and honorable people in the city where we reside; we can hold that there is nothing just, divine or ultimate in the world. In so living we help to create the despair and destruction inherent in their opposites.

On the other hand, we can believe in the goodness of

things. Even when afflictions assail us, we can live "as if" the kindly and hopeful virtues were true. Our beliefs, translated into action, help to make reality of that in which we hold faith.

For instance, when the lawyer received such unjust treatment from the politician and from his law partners, he was faced with several alternatives. He could react with bitterness, resentment and hostility. He could allow the incidents to become the hinge of a broken and defeated personality. He could decide that all men were cruel and deceitful. Resolved not to receive a similar injury again, he could stifle the humane impulses within and face the future with suspicion and ruthlessness. Living "as if" the response he selected were proper and true, it would be true for him; ultimately it would shape him into the kind of person he pictured, a cynical, bitter, defeated man.

On the other hand, he could face the incidents objectively and determine not to allow them to defeat him or to turn him sour. Recognizing the unfairness in that which happened to him, he could refuse to believe that this was the standard pattern of human conduct. He could close the door on self-pity and resentment, and resolve to take from the situation only that which would enrich his personality and make him a stronger, deeper, more understanding man. He could hold confidence that these keen disappointments could fit him for a wider opportunity which lay ahead. Living "as if" such conduct were possible in the situation and that such faith were justified, they would prove so for him. His faith would mold him into a far different—and far more mature—type of personality than if he had chosen to believe in suspicion, hostility and callousness.

In the midst of discouragement and doubt, or in the face of similar injustice, if we have faith to live "as if" goodness, righteousness and love were the higher attributes of character—putting our belief into creative action—our discouragement will lift and our doubts will lighten. Also, the impact of our lives will help to build the thing in which we hold faith. If we can believe, like Tennyson, that a loving purpose hallows each unselfish service and that not a single act of forgiveness or compassion

> . . . shall be destroy'd,
> Or cast as rubbish to the void
> When God hath made the pile complete,

our action will help to make it so. In this confused and fear-ridden world, it is possible that one of the highest functions of our lives is to live up to our "as if's."

William James, the pioneer psychologist, illustrates the principle. He pictures a man who comes to a wide crevasse as he climbs a mountain. His situation is such that he cannot turn back, so his only possibility is to leap over the crevasse. If he has faith that he can do so and leaps confidently into the air, arching the abyss below, he has a greater likelihood of landing safely on the far side to continue his climb. If, on the other hand, he doubts of his ability to leap the chasm, if he is sure that he will fail and tells himself that he will fall, the chances are strong that when at last he launches himself into the air with a terrible despair, the man will tumble into the abyss, the victim of his doubts. This principle being true, it is wise to doubt our doubts and to believe our beliefs. Success, power and happiness lie in that direction.

Suppose that we are asked to assume a new position. Perhaps in our imagination we accentuate the magnitude and complexity of its duties and we doubt that our abilities can measure up. We tell ourselves, "It looks as if I cannot handle it; it is too much for me. I know that I shall fail." If we accept the responsibility while holding such an attitude, we already have increased our chance of failure. When, by our doubts, we limit what we *can* do, we limit what we *will* do.

Now imagine that we approach this same responsibility in a positive spirit. We do not minimize the difficulties in the situation or underestimate its complexities. We study our own capacities objectively, neither egotistically nor falsely humble. We see the new position as an opportunity to expand our abilities and to increase our usefulness. After having checked, analyzed and counted the cost, we accept the responsibility. We have greatly increased our chances of success because of our affirmative approach; our faith works *for* us, not against us. We can launch ourselves confidently over the abyss toward this new undertaking, powered with the trust that we will continue to climb on the other side.

Doubt is a destroyer, while faith is a builder. Every advance in the field of exploration, science, industry, social interrelatedness or successful personal living is *an act of faith and a triumphant conquest of doubt.*

Clearly, humankind cannot be explained on the physical level alone. Man is akin to the animals, but he is something more—he possesses intangibles. True, he can outbrutalize the beast, as we learn from Robert Burns—"man's inhumanity to man makes countless thousands mourn"—but even in his beastliness, he knows it. Man thinks and his thoughts build cities, hurl airplanes into the stratosphere, spawn industries and shape inventions of amazing cleverness. His thoughts are creative forces, although no one ever has seen a thought. Man has courage which will cast him unflinchingly into hellish dangers and lead him to acts of Godlike heroism, but no one ever has seen courage. Man has patriotism which guides him into acts of selfless devotion, but no one ever has seen patriotism. He has personality, purpose, ambition, yet no one ever has seen any of them—only their evidence.

Beyond question man cannot be explained on the physical level alone. He walks more by insight than by sight. He lives by faith in something; even when he denies faith he does not escape faith. He merely exchanges a positive for a negative faith. If he believes that he has no faith, *he still uses the faith faculty to believe it*. Faith is inherent in man's psychological structure. He does not have to discover it; he needs only to exercise it constructively.

The faith faculty must be nurtured, disciplined, trained, or in the hour of crisis it collapses through lack of stamina. What would happen to a professional boxer who went into the ring without long hours of training behind him? What would be his chances of beating a tough and wily opponent? Having been knocked out, would he have the right to complain that his muscles had proved traitorous because they had not carried him to victory? Yet, unthinkingly, we assume such an attitude toward our personal faith. The world against which we pit our strength today is a tough-handed and merciless opponent. If we are to triumph it will demand the best of the intelligence, stamina and skill that we can muster. It will take training and discipline; yet we overlook the necessity to exercise our faith in constructive channels. We assume that, because it is inherent, faith always will be powerful and poised whenever we may have occasion to call on it in urgent need. Then when it is not vigorous enough to meet the challenge of a critical hour, we are bewildered and chagrined. Declaring that faith has failed us, we turn our backs on faith.

Dean James Currie McLeod of Northwestern University told of an incident which occurred in the lounge car of a train. A group of businessmen had gathered there and he was seated among them. The conversation turned to world affairs. One man voiced his personal conviction of the danger that communism held for the world in general and for our nation in particular. He cited some of the ruthless methods the Communists had employed against their own people. "Why," he exclaimed, "they have even closed the churches!"

Dean McLeod asked him, "By the way, of what church are you a member?"

The man hesitated a moment, then answered, "Well, I'm not actually a member of any church."

"Have you attended church recently?" the dean pursued with a smile.

"No," he replied. "As a matter of fact, I haven't gone to church for some time. My wife sees that the children get to Sunday School, but Sunday is the only day I have to rest. I like to play golf or putter around the house; I don't go to church."

Dean McLeod then asked, "What right have you to talk about closing the churches in Russia? From firsthand experience, you can't tell if the churches are open here in the United States!"

Under this frank criticism, the man bristled for an instant. Then, with a typical American sense of fair play, he relaxed, smiled and admitted that the dean had a point.

The dean did have a point. To be sure, loyalty to the church or synagogue and regularity at worship are not all there is to the nurture of personal faith, but these help to keep our spirits sensitive and our wills dedicated to transcendant values.

The third chapter of the Book of Daniel tells of three heroes of the faith, Shadrach, Meshach and Abednego. When these men were carried into captivity, they did not forget their God, but continued to practice the disciplines of their religion. The king built a golden idol and they were commanded to worship it or to suffer the death penalty. Their faith held steady and they refused to bow before the idol. Having sentenced them to death in the fiery furnace, the king taunted them, "Who is the god that will deliver you out of my hands?"

The young men made this ringing answer, "Our God

whom we serve is able to deliver us from the burning fiery furnace. . . . *But if not,* be it known unto thee, O king, that we will not serve thy gods, nor worship the golden image which thou hast set up." In happier times they had learned that the Lord was their Shepherd, a present Help in the time of trouble. But if in the day of trial He did not answer their prayers and come to save them, they would not give up faith, drop their loyalties and worship at pagan altars. They still would trust where they could not see.

"There must be a nightingale in every forest," says the Voice in Edmond Rostand's *Chantecler.* "And in the soul," cries Chantecler with exultation, "there must always be a faith so sure of itself that it comes back even after it has been slain." Such magnificent faith does not develop without effort. Like every cherished value, it is bought at the cost of discipline, testing and experience.

CHAPTER V

Where the "Practical" Man Loses Out

SINCE a working faith, as discussed in the preceding chapter, is essential to a successful quest for personal happiness, there is small wonder that the loss of peace of mind and the rise of ennui and dissatisfaction have paralleled a growth of skepticism and withered faith. Such skepticism has expressed itself in a type of practical atheism which has settled over our present age like the smog that blankets a city. Urbane, morally upright people have divorced themselves from religion because they are convinced that religion is an antiquated and sentimental appendage which, in a streamlined age, they can readily discard. Many of these people are cultured, attractive, educated and possess a ready kindness. But for a variety of reasons modern faith has failed to challenge their interest or capture their wills. As a consequence, religious observance or the application of religious insights to their personal problems has no place in their lives.

One has a lively respect and sympathy for such individuals, but the fact remains that they fail to understand the impact and the power of religious truth in relation to their day and to their thirst for wholeness, stability and peace. They have ignored the relevancy of religious insights to the mental, emotional and spiritual needs of modern man. Materially comfortable, professionally successful, socially acceptable, they still are dissatisfied. The deep contentments and the enduring joys somehow have eluded them. It seems apparent that the "practical" man, ethically sound and with much to admire, yet wistful and unhappy, is fooling himself as he never would allow himself to be duped in his business or profession.

He is fooling himself, first of all, about the nature and function of religion. He is confused as to what religion is or what it does, although he may assume that he understands enough about religion for all practical purposes. Often this is because he holds a childhood conception of Christianity. Probably he was reared in a devout home, nurtured in the Sunday School, the youth fellowship and other training activities of the church. Unconsciously he still conceives of religion in terms which he understood in childhood and, finding such religious ideas inadequate for his adult experience, he discards them as being impractical. As a child, perhaps he thought of God as an aged man. As he grew, his mental horizons expanded. Since a fatherly God seated on a throne did not square with scientific facts, God lost intimacy for him, then reality. Gradually he pushed Deity off into infinite space until finally he doubted that God existed.

He learned that universal laws control the physical world. These natural laws seemed to leave no place for prayer. He asked himself why God—if there were a God—should suspend natural law or rearrange His order of things to cater to man's personal whims. At the best, prayer came to mean little more than autosuggestion.

In like manner, the Bible became suspect. It pictured another world of long ago, strikingly different from his modern, mechanized, twentieth-century world. It was a flat earth. At a man's demand the sun stood still. Angels appeared and disappeared, animals spoke with human voices, ax heads floated in the water, God spoke with men and men with God, and perplexing things were said and done which have no counterpart in modern experience.

Thus, one after another, he discards his beliefs. Religion becomes "impractical." The obvious explanation is that religiously the man stopped growing in childhood or adolescence. He grew mentally, he matured physically, but religiously he remained immature. He could not say with St. Paul, "When I was a child, I spake as a child, I understood as a child, I thought as a child: but when I became a man, I put away childish things." Sam Walter Foss, in "The Two Gods," depicts this failure to grow spiritually.

A boy was born 'mid little things,
    Between a little world and sky—
And dreamed not of the cosmic rings
    Round which the circling planets fly.

He lived in little works and thoughts,
    Where little ventures grow and plod,
And paced and ploughed his little plots,
    And prayed unto his little God.

But as the mighty system grew,
    His faith grew faint with many scars;
The Cosmos widened in his view—
    But God was lost among His stars.

Another boy in lowly days,
    As he, to little things was born,
But gathered lore in woodland ways,
    And from the glory of the morn.

As wider skies broke on his view,
    God greatened in his growing mind;
Each year he dreamed his God anew,
    And left his older God behind.

He saw the boundless scheme dilate,
    In star and blossom, sky and clod;
And as the universe grew great,
    He dreamed for it a greater God.[1]

The practical man, like the first boy pictured, loses God among the stars. Not having allowed his faith to keep pace with his growing factual knowledge, religion becomes weak and ineffectual.

He fails to understand that prayer is not an attempt to wheedle a reluctant God into granting individual favors. Neither is it a clumsy attempt to wield spiritual magic. Rather, prayer is intelligent co-operation with spiritual laws, a co-operation which allows the Divine to channel spiritual forces into the world through human lives.

The practical man has not learned to appreciate the Bible for what it is. It is not intended to be a scientific handbook, a guide to biology, astronomy or physics. It is a spiritual biography of the race, revealing Deity's dealings with man and man's response to the Divine. It is a revelation of God's yearning and need for His human children, and of their growing awareness and response to that love. It is a record of man's long, slow struggle upward toward the spiritual aspirations which haunt and challenge humankind. It is a book of practical spiritual formulas which, when applied, bring personal poise and peace. It reveals the true nature of God and lays bare universal spiritual laws as objective and real as those which govern the physical world.

If it were not for his spiritual immaturity the urbane, practical man would sense that many of the shortcomings which he attributes to religion are housed within himself.

In the second place, the practical man is likely to declare that he is "too busy for religion." Actually, this means that religion has lost its sense of value for him. We find time, as a rule, for the things in which we are most interested and which we believe to be of worth. When we eliminate religion, it means that we do not consider it of primary value. Al-Ghazzali, the Moslem mystic, goes to the heart of the matter: "If you are never alone with God, it is not because

you are too busy; it is because you don't care for him. And
you had better face the facts." The facts are that when life
becomes so preoccupied as to leave no room for spiritual
concern, it drifts into the shallows and suffers danger of
shipwreck. When an individual gets "too busy"—making
money, having a good time, or frittering away hours and
abilities in trivialities—and has slender time left for the deep
and abiding values on which the satisfactions of life ultimately depend, that person is fooling himself. "We look not
at the things which are seen," the Apostle Paul wisely declares, "but at the things which are not seen: for the things
which are seen are temporal; but the things which are not
seen are eternal." The emphasis should lie there.

Religion grants worth-while causes to which to attach our
allegiance. At its minimum, it keeps sympathy and compassion alive. Our lives expand as they enter into fellowship and
co-operation with others. *"Unus homo, nullus homo,"* the
Romans put it pointedly—man alone is no man at all. Here
the irreligious personality loses out. He becomes so absorbed
in himself and in superficial values that he loses sensitivity
to the needs of others.

When a person becomes so self-centered and impervious
to the feelings of those about him that he loses his capacity
to "feel with"—as the word "sympathy" means—thus resembling a stone wall or the head of a hammer, he has placed
himself in an unenviable position. Presumably there is no
one who in his best moments does not wish to do some good
in the world, to make his life count beyond himself. A man
finds opportunity at his own doorstep to be of help to others,
if he is not too busy or self-concerned to notice. Few exer-
cises are more rewarding than to reach down to give someone
a lift, and few sources are richer in peace and personal satisfaction. By a universal law, those who give consideration and
love to others receive an ever-increasing supply of love and

happiness in return; the store does not diminish, but rather grows. The practical man runs the risk of missing this satisfaction when he becomes so busy that he rules religion out of his life.

The practical man loses out, in the third place, when his convictions lead him to the point where he rejects the spiritual interpretation of life. "I am a realist," he declares. "There is too much vagueness and unreality in religion to suit me, too much dependence on things which you cannot verify. I accept only that which I can prove—that which I can handle, smell, see, hear or taste. All I believe is what I know with my five senses. I am a practical man."

If we limit the world to the slender store of experience that our five senses can transmit, the universe in which we live is narrow indeed. Shortly after a spectacular solar eclipse, a forest ranger fell into conversation with a young mountaineer. When the talk drifted to the eclipse, the young man showed a lively interest. "What happened to the sun the other day?" he inquired.

The ranger explained the eclipse to him in terms of the Copernican theory of earth and sun, and the backwoodsman shook his head incredulously.

"I don't believe it!" he said. "I don't believe the earth is round, in the first place."

"Do you mean that you think the earth is flat?" asked the ranger. The mountaineer made what seemed to him a conclusive reply:

"Well, every place I ever was it has been flat!"

Anyone who attempts to define life in terms of personal experience and by the evidence of the senses is bound by the same limitations. The truth is that man does not live by physical proof. He does not narrow his experience to the five senses. He lives not by sight alone, but by insight. Penicillin and sulpha kill infection through different attacks, but when we are ill we do not demand a scientific explanation of how either drug works. We accept it on faith—faith in the doctor, faith in his assurance that it will aid us, and faith in the experience of others who have taken the drugs and have been helped by them. When we switch on the electric toaster in the morning, we do so without a complete understanding of the nature of electricity. No one comprehends electricity completely. Scientists have acquired a tremendous store of knowledge about it. They know the rules which govern its use, but they do not know what electricity *is*. It does not follow that we have no toast for breakfast. We do not demand an exhaustive explanation of electricity; we *use* it, accepting it through faith and past experience.

Life's deepest values are received on the same basis. When a man falls in love with the girl of his dreams, he does not demand proof that she will make an ideal wife, an immaculate housekeeper, a model hostess and a worthy mother of his children before asking her to be his bride. He does not insist that she sign a legal document stating that she will never cease to be even-tempered and sweet, without major faults, and with unswerving admiration for the perfect man who is her husband. If such proof were required beforehand, marriages would be made only in heaven! But faith and love have their own rewards and, like many precious values in life, are not subject to scientific proof.

Suppose that we walk into the Sistine Chapel and our souls are awed by the grandeur of its frescoes. We exclaim, "What magnificent painting!" Some shallow person whose idea of art is the comic section of the Sunday paper challenges us: "What do you mean when you say that this is great painting? Prove it to me!" What explanation can we give to one so dull of insight and appreciation? We can point out certain evidences, but proof limps and falls. It is not

possible to measure beauty by mathematics or to test it with
a slide rule.

We listen breathlessly to a Beethoven symphony, or thrill
to Handel's *Messiah*. We remark, "That is glorious music!"
An exponent of "bebop" wants to know, "What is thrilling
about it? It doesn't 'send' me. Prove it!" What can we answer
that will make sense to such a person?

We turn in the Bible to one of the Psalms, to a section of
St. John's gospel, or to one of the matchless passages of the
prophets. As we read, something in our souls rises in response and we declare, "This is sublime! This is eternal!" A
critic demands, "Prove to me, if you can, that the Bible is
superior to any other book. What I read in it doesn't help
me cut out a dress, bake a cake, or improve my skill at the
bridge table. It doesn't aid me to maneuver a sharp deal or
to outsmart my competitors. Prove its sublimity!" What have
we to say in reply? The sweetest and deepest values of life
are not experienced through media subject to physical proof.
They enter through the channels of insight, faith and appreciation. This is where the person who prides himself as a
realist is likely to lose out. We can but feel pity that he
misses so much.

Furthermore, on what inner resources can the superficial
life call in the hour of personal crisis? When life caves in,
what then? A man lives on the sunny side of Easy Street.
Not a cloud mars his sky. Then the winds turn chill and the
storm rolls in. His children turn out bad, he meets financial
reverses and ill health. The security built up through a lifetime disappears. Where can he find a solid foundation to
steady his house of life? A woman centers her life around a
son; suddenly the boy dies. What spiritual support has she
to bridge the awful chasm of despair and grief?

The name of the man and woman is legion. Having cut
themselves off from the securities and comforts of faith, they

meet the extremities of life with meager resources. Some curse fate and accept their losses with bitterness. Some limp through existence with broken spirits. Some whimper "Why?" and consume themselves with self-pity. At best, some meet disaster with stoical endurance. They allow themselves small chance to plant the saving seeds of faith and hope that can mature into a harvest of acceptance and peace. In this, the practical man penalizes himself. His own resources are not sufficient to meet all the experiences that life may thrust on him.

Karl Marx once wrote, "Philosophers have only interpreted the world differently, but the point is to change it." His mistake was in the methods he used and the goal toward which he directed the change. The Master of the spiritual life subscribed to the same conviction. He was not afraid of skepticism or earnest doubt. "Ye shall know the truth," he said, "and the truth shall set you free." Through the realistic ventures of life, grimy with frustration and gritty with pain, we can prove in our own experience the validity of who he was and of what he said.

On the eastern seaboard, so I have read, a boy was talking with an old sailor. Finally the boy asked this hard question, "What is the wind?"

The old salt squinted at the sky for a long moment before he answered. "Son," he said, "I can't tell you what the wind is, but I can hoist a sail!"

If you are among those who feel that religion is not practical and therefore does not matter, or that happiness has little to do with an inner sense of values, it is well to remember that there is no pat formula to answer life's deepest questions. "What is the wind?" Spiritually, no one can determine that for you; the eternal winds of the spirit blow where they will. But you can hoist a sail. Try it and see!

CHAPTER VI

Making the Most of Our Abilities

A MAN once wrote to a person whom he admired greatly, congratulating him on his amazing abilities. The letter he received in reply contained these sentences:

No, my friend, you are quite wrong about me. I am just an ordinary individual, without special ability in any line. In most things I am only just above the average; in some things I am under the average rather than over. This is certainly true of my physical powers. I can't run, I'm only an ordinary walker, I'm certainly not a good swimmer. I can probably ride a horse better than I can do anything else, but I am not a remarkable horseman. Neither am I a good shot. My eyesight is so poor that I have to be near my game to take any aim at all. So you can see that, as far as physical gifts are concerned, I am just an ordinary man. The same thing is true of my literary ability. I am certainly not a brilliant writer. During my lifetime I have written a good deal, but I always have to work and slave over everything I put on paper.

Who was this man of ordinary abilities who had done so much with them that he had excited the admiration of others? His name was Theodore Roosevelt. By his own judgment, he was a man of no outstanding talents—but how he used the abilities he had! This brings into focus a question which troubles many of us. What is the secret which harnesses ordinary powers to outstanding achievements? How do some individuals attract admiration for extraordinary results when actually they possess only limited talent?

Over nineteen hundred years ago, Jesus of Nazareth told a parable that has bearing on the question. "A man going on a journey called his servants and entrusted to them his property; to one he gave five talents, to another two, to another one, to each according to his ability. Then he went away." The three men cast about for ways to employ the talents entrusted to their care. In imagination, it is possible to follow their actions.

The man who received five talents was resourceful and intelligent. He followed with keen interest the reports of growing drought in Syria; studied the weather, the soil and the chances for good crops; became acquainted with the leading merchants in the caravans from Damascus and Antioch; and made shrewd judgments on the prospects of war or peace. On the basis of such information he placed his five talents to the best advantage, with the result that he realized 100 per cent gain on his transactions. The second man, entrusted with two talents, was not as perceptive as the first, but he was honest and industrious. The rising sun found him in field or vineyard, and when it sank in the west he still plodded persistently at his tasks. He drove himself and his oxen hard and thus he made his two talents yield two talents more. The third servant differed from the other two. Fearful and unimaginative, he did not try to expand his single talent by effort of either mind or muscle. His timidity and lack of vision caused him to bury his talent in the earth.

When the owner returned, he commended the two faithful servants who had doubled the talents entrusted to them, the man who earned two talents receiving equal praise with the man who had gained five. But the master sternly rebuked the servant who had hidden his talent and had not put it to use. "Take the talent from him," he commanded, "and give it to him who has the ten talents." Thus the man lost even the single talent he had.

Think of the word "talent" as synonymous with "ability" and several suggestions on how to make the most of our capabilities rise out of this ancient story. The first is to *take stock of our abilities*. What talents do we possess? What are our assets, our strong points? We should also take our inclinations into account. Possibly we have several talents, any one of which could develop into something useful and satisfying if we were to pursue it; our inclination helps us decide which of our assets to develop. A mother asked her little boy, "Tommy, would you rather go shopping with me this afternoon, or would you rather visit your Aunt Mary?" The little fellow answered, "Well, if I had my *druthers*, I'd druther go swimming." If we had our *druthers* of what to do with our abilities, what would we choose? A talk with a wise friend, a clergyman, a banker, a lawyer, or a vocational counselor may help. Perhaps we should take vocational guidance tests to reveal our potentials. Such consultation and analysis should aid in determining the area in which we should strive to use our abilities.

In taking stock of our abilities, we should ask ourselves if the area in which we have talent is feasible. A man who once was a member of Admiral Richard E. Byrd's Arctic expedition fell in love with the Far North. He still dreams of his experiences on that expedition. He wants to dedicate his life to polar explorations, but the ambition hardly is practical —there is a dearth of polar expeditions at present. Because he cannot fulfill his heart's desire, he is discontented and unco-operative in the work he does; frankly he makes himself a nuisance. Instead of dreaming about exploring the Arctic, would it not be more sensible to explore the needs of his neighborhood and to organize a restless young group of vandals into a boys' club, or to use his fine abilities—and he

has them—in leading a Boy Scout troop? He could fire growing boys with admiration for the kind of bravery, team play,
unselfishness and integrity essential to the conquest of the
polar regions—and of their own futures.

We should apply the same test to ourselves, if we are in
earnest about making the most of our abilities. Is our ambition feasible? Does it lie in the range of practical possibility?
If not, we are wise to turn our aspirations to other channels.
We should begin by surveying the opportunities open to us.
Situations which at first appear as roadblocks may later reveal themselves as walls of guidance.

On a train trip west, I was attracted to a clean-cut Negro
porter and struck up a conversation with him. He inquired
about the opportunities to study pharmacy in Chicago.

"I'm a student in the University of Arizona," he said, "but
it doesn't offer some of the courses I need."

"How did you decide on pharmacy as a career?" I asked
him.

"I really wanted to study medicine," he explained, "but it
is hard to break into the field, for the medical schools are so
crowded that it is next to impossible to receive an appointment. I also thought of dentistry, but the situation is much
the same. Good pharmacists are greatly needed and I believe
that I can offer real service in that profession."

The young man was hitching his wagon of purpose to a
practical star. He was matching his aspirations realistically
with opportunity. Denied his first choice, and even his second, this did not deter him from expanding his abilities into
practical and highly useful service.

A second suggestion is to *discipline our abilities for maximum usefulness.* Success demands foresight and industry. It
responds to thought and care. Thorough preparation is im-
perative if we are to use our capabilities to the fullest. The
greatest undiscovered resources in the world lie under our

hats and stand in our shoes. It is our responsibility to develop
them.

Someone receives a promotion, gets an important assignment, makes a major discovery, or moves into the president's
office. "He was lucky," an envious person remarks. "He gets
the breaks; they're always in his favor." In reality, luck or
the breaks of life had little or nothing to do with it. So-called
"luck" usually is found at the exact point where preparation
meets opportunity. For a time, an individual may get ahead
by "pull," but eventually someone with push will displace
him. Success is not due to a fortuitous concourse of stars at
our birth, but to a steady trail of sparks from the grindstone
of hard work each day.

"Babe" Didrickson Zaharias has been called the athletic
phenomenon of all time. This woman from Texas ran,
jumped, rode and played such contact games as basketball
and baseball with superb skill. Her prowess in track and field
events won five first places in the Olympic tryouts in 1932,
and made her an international sensation when in the Olympic
games in Los Angeles that same year she placed first in the
women's eighty meter hurdles, first in the javelin throw, and
second in the high jump. Then she turned to golf. When she
won the National Woman's Amateur and the British Woman's Amateur championships, certain people said, "It was
inevitable. She is just a natural athlete. She is an automatic
champion."

The facts, however, tell a different story about the "automatic champion." When the "Babe" took up golf she sought
an exceptionally fine instructor to teach her. She studied the
game. She analyzed the golf swing, dissected it and tested
each component part until she felt that she understood it
thoroughly. When she went on a practice tee she would
practice as much as twelve hours a day, hitting as many as
one thousand balls in an afternoon. She would swing and

keep swinging until her hands were so sore that she scarcely could grip a club. She would stop swinging long enough to tape her hands before picking up her club again. That is the method she used to perfect her powerful swing.

Does that sound as if she were an automatic champion? It takes preparation, training and hard work to become a champion in any field of athletics. More recently, her courageous battle against cancer, exhibiting the same high qualities of courage, perseverance and faith, has won the admiration of a nation. Mrs. Zaharias subscribes to the theory that in order to make the most of one's abilities, one must prepare diligently to use them.

A definite *sense of purpose* also adds a strong motivation toward making the most of our abilities. It is doubtful that Mrs. Zaharias would have worked seriously to perfect her golf game if she had not had a flaming desire to play championship golf. Nor will we cultivate and develop our capacities to their fullest until a compelling purpose inspires us to do so. We all know that purpose makes a difference; a clear picture of what we wish to accomplish and the determination to reach our goal strengthens our power to achieve it. It can make the difference between success and failure, frustration and zest for living, happiness and unhappiness. Strong lives are motivated by dynamic purposes; lesser ones exist on wishes and inclinations. The most glowing successes are but the reflections of an inner fire.

The biography of Mme. Curie, written by her daughter, depicts her long struggle to discover radium. After her husband Pierre and she had become convinced that radium existed, they struggled four long, grueling years in their shed laboratory—years filled with perplexities and bitter disappointments—in an effort to isolate radium. With a terrible patience they treated tons of pitchblende residue kilogram by kilogram, certain that it contained radium. Experiment after experiment failed. In the film version, after the forty-eighth experiment was unsuccessful, her husband gave way to despair. "It can't be done," he cried, "it can't be done! Maybe in a hundred years it can be done, but never in our lifetime." Mme. Curie was made of sterner stuff. "If it takes a hundred years it will be a pity," she answered, "but I dare not do less than work for it so long as I have life." [1]

Confronted by such a sense of purpose, the mysteries surrounding radium finally gave way on a night which she was to remember always as a night of magic. She had spent the earlier part of the evening with an ill child. When at last the little one slept, she said to her husband, "Suppose we go down there for a moment?" A note of supplication was in her voice—a superfluous note, for Pierre was as eager as she. Arm in arm they went through the streets to the shed. "Don't light the lamps," she said to Pierre as he unlocked the door. Then she added with a little laugh, "Do you remember the day when you said to me, 'I should like radium to be a beautiful color'?" They stepped into the room and an indescribably beautiful bluish glow lighted the darkness. Wordlessly they looked at the pale, glimmering, mysterious source of radiation—radium, their radium, the reward of their resolution and patient labor.

Multitudes of people, drifting aimlessly to and fro without a set purpose, deny themselves such fulfillment of their capacities, and the satisfying happiness which attends it. They are not wicked; they are only shallow. They are not mean or vicious; they simply are empty—shake them and they would rattle like gourds. They lack range, depth and conviction. Without purpose their lives ultimately wander into the morass of dissatisfaction.

As we harness our abilities to a steady purpose and undertake the long pull toward its accomplishment, rich compensations reward us. A sense of purpose simplifies life and therefore concentrates our abilities; and concentration adds power. King Edward VII of England once asked General William Booth, founder of the Salvation Army, how he could give himself with utter devotion to such an exacting—and often thankless—task. General Booth's reply is revealing:

> Some men's passion is gold.
> Some men's passion is fame.
> My passion is souls.

The concentration of his will toward serving dejected humanity gave power to his capacities.

Jane Addams, founder of Hull House in Chicago and world benefactress, discovered the purpose of her life at an early age. When only six, she glimpsed the destitution and squalor in the back streets of Freeport, Illinois. The sight impressed her so deeply that she insisted that, when she grew up, she would have a big house like the one in which she lived, only it would stand among little houses like those she had seen. The sense of compassion never deserted her. It became the focal point of her abilities, and Hull House became the big friendly house standing in the midst of little houses, fulfilling her childhood dream. But would Jane Addams ever have become Jane Addams without her sense of purpose, or would Hull House ever have been born? Without a corresponding sense of purpose, can *we* reach the levels of attainment which lie within our powers to achieve? Sustained by such a purpose, will any hardship thwart or deter us? Consult some difficult chapter in your personal experience for the answer, perhaps your struggle to gain an education. You had to make your own way financially and the going was hard. You received little help, except from your own two hands—and your will to succeed. You did without many things the other students had and there were periods when you did not think that you would be able to pull through, but somehow you did. The proud day finally arrived when, with your mortarboard on your head and your gown draped around your shoulders, you waved your sheepskin triumphantly and shouted, "I have done it!"

You would not wish to go through that trying period again, but is it not true that some of the most precious personal values you then received would not be yours if the way had been easy and the road smooth? Your talents were tempered and expanded. You learned patience and endurance—and the value of money. The sacrifices you were called to make proved worth-while and you do not regret the hardships you endured. The lesson is clear: in whatever area we may wish to apply our abilities and to find the happiness of personal accomplishment, we must be willing to sacrifice for the expansion of our talents.

Having taken stock of our inclinations and abilities, and having prepared them for use in the light of a compelling purpose, the next step is to *put our talents to work*. In using them we develop them. Even if our abilities seem small to us, or the opportunity to use them seems insignificant, it is important to exercise them to the fullest. The third servant in the parable was condemned, not because he had used his talent for an evil purpose, but because he had failed to use it at all. That was his shortcoming.

The practical truth of this insight is demonstrated all about us. People with ordinary talents often achieve more than those with greater physical and intellectual endowments because they work harder with what they have. In the ancient story of the hare and the tortoise, the hare could run much faster than the tortoise. He had far more ability. Yet the tortoise won the race because he used his ability to the utmost. He kept plodding toward the goal, while the hare dallied along the way. "The race is not always to the swift," nor do achievement and success always accrue to those with the nimblest wits and the highest I. Q.'s. Many individuals fail to achieve success for the same reason that Jim did not become wealthy in the gold rush days. Jim remained a ne'er-do-well in the midst of riches. A friend explained, "Jim has the gold fever, but he doesn't have the digging principle." We should not acquiesce as easily. For our own good, we should scorn the easy way and the second best; the "digging principle" is important! When we match our abilities against something hard each day, some task that seems beyond our capacity, we are exercising will, mind and body to good purpose. As we master hard things we gain the ability to handle still more difficult assignments and fuller responsibilities. As we struggle, we grow. After Paderewski played before Queen Victoria, the sovereign exclaimed enthusiastically, "Mr. Paderewski, you are a genius!" "Ah, Your Majesty," he replied, "perhaps; but before I was a genius I was a drudge."

In putting our talents to work, *imagination* adds amazing outreach to our capacities. It opens doors of achievement and happiness which we do not anticipate and which once we would have believed to be beyond our wildest hopes of attainment. The power of imagination is one of man's greatest assets, one of the qualities which makes him unique. Think of attempting to turn a stubborn nut from a bolt with only your thumb and forefinger. Ages ago, after the discovery of the lever and the wheel, some imaginative genius fashioned an extension of the thumb and forefinger; the first wrench was born, and today specialized tools do the work of many powerful hands. Imagine trying to drive a spike with your clenched fist. Creative individuals in the distant past put their imaginations to work on the problem; first they used a convenient stone to drive a primitive peg, then devised a crude hammer. Thus man's strength was multiplied. Imagination was fascinated by fire, and the internal combustion engine captured its flame. Imagination watched steam, and the steam engine became the servant of mankind. Imagination saw mechanical fingers sorting seeds from cotton pods, dreamed of writing not done by hand that could be multiplied, envisioned mechanical means to sow and reap grain, harnessed the lightning, flung heavier-than-air machines into the air, and finally split the atom to release its power. From one step to another, imagination has led mankind to the heights of achievement. It has produced every article we use, made every discovery for the betterment of our health and comfort, built every church and institution, and sponsored the manifold complexities of modern civilization. It is the priceless ingredient of moral, sociological and scientific advance, a better day, and a happier personal life. Imagination is creative, as industry is fully aware. The Aluminum Company of America has coined a new word—"imagineering." The company explains that in imagineering "you let your imagination soar and then engineer it down to earth."

We are wise to apply the same principle in the use of our abilities. Said Marcus Aurelius, "As thy thoughts are so will thy mind be also: for the soul takes its coloring from thought." [2] When we fail to use imagination, our lives become routine. Routine leads to a rut of complacency, and complacency is deadly to the creative expansion of our skills. Imagination looks at each situation with fresh eyes and discovers possibilities hitherto unseen. A little French girl, for instance, the daughter of a poor Parisian, had prayed for money to hire a model to pose for her; she had been born almost with a paint brush in her hand, and painting was her consuming passion. But no francs fell in the back yard in answer to her earnest prayers. Then one day, while she was taking a walk in the market place, she called on her imagination to answer her problem—and there he was, standing strong and still before her, waiting to be painted! She had found her model—a farmer's horse! He would not mind posing for her, she was sure, if she did not mind painting him. In a flurry of excitement, she rushed for her easel and brushes. Today, in the Metropolitan Museum of Art in New York City, we can view a famous canvas entitled "The Horse Fair," painted by Rosa Bonheur, noted for her masterly painting of horses.

Imagination can overcome our difficulties, open dead-end streets, give fresh and creative outlets for our talents, expand our contribution to society and, in so doing, increase our store of personal happiness. Whatever our individual situation may be, once we loose our imagination like a bird dog in an open field, sniffing every scent and following each trail until coming to a point before a fresh idea, our capabilities are bound to deepen and enrich. What we can imagine, we can achieve—if we are willing to "engineer it down to earth." Imagination places a future in our minds, a future which challenges our aptitudes and draws forth the best that lies within us. We cannot rise above the level of our vision. The man who guides a pushcart through the alleys to pick up bottles and stray bits of paper will remain between the shafts of his rickety cart as long as his vision rises no higher than collecting scraps. The derelict on "Skid Row" will remain a derelict until a vision grips him to aspire to a finer destiny. Imagination hangs pictures in the gallery of our minds, pictures which can lure us to our best attainments and which, in our struggle toward them, comfort us with encouragement and hope.

The lack of education has little to do with the vital use of imagination; we cannot excuse ourselves on that score. In fact, some educational procedures seem to hinder, rather than to aid, creativity and make it sterile. Our imaginations stem from our emotions and our wills more than from knowledge formally acquired. People who have enjoyed little formal education are among the most creative, those who have achieved outstanding results. The Wildroot Company, as Alex Osborn has explained, is a monument to men without schooling; it was founded by two barbers, Robert Kideney and Morrel Howe, who worked at adjoining chairs in the Old Iroquois Hotel in Buffalo, New York. They had little schooling but they had alert imaginations. The same company attained national prominence through Harry James Lehman's creative leadership; he was driving a junk wagon for his uncle when other boys his age were in high school. The Lane Bryant Company was first a dream in the fertile mind of Lena Himmelstein, who came from Russia as an immigrant girl of sixteen. The list could be multiplied. Our basic trouble is never limited education, but limited vision; not lack of dexterity, but lack of daring; not too little competence, but too little trust.

Imagination is important. So is *enthusiasm*. In the parable, the man who hid his talent in the earth lacked both. Even a superficial study of successful personalities reveals that without exception they are imbued with enthusiasm for their work and are alive with ideas for the future. They are excited about what they are doing, and they communicate the excitement to others. Their abilities take on a powerful thrust which they would lack without it. One of the remarkable business leaders in our generation, for instance, is Conrad Hilton, head of a mammoth chain of hotels around the world. His life reads like a Horatio Alger story. Literally from thirty-five cents in cash and an indebtedness of half a million dollars he has built a multimillion dollar corporation in a quarter of a century. There are many facets to such a versatile and energetic personality, but one of the fundamental forces motivating his success is enthusiasm. One senses and is attracted to this dynamic quality about him after being with him only a brief time.

"Since my earliest recollection," Mr. Hilton wrote, "I have been fortunate in the possession of enthusiasm. With enthusiasm as a base and prayer as a buttress, I have liked my life. The probabilities are that this kind of equipment leads directly to a full and happy life. . . . Most certainly I believe in courage and enthusiasm, for without them the individual is hampering his own desired wishes." [3]

Most of us cannot aspire to Mr. Hilton's dramatic success as a hotelier, but we can strive to produce in ourselves similar courage, faith, vision and enthusiasm. Such qualities are invaluable as they relate to the productive use of our individual talents. All of us are enthusiastic at times. Some of us retain our eagerness for an hour, a day, a week or a month. But if we can sustain enthusiasm indefinitely, honestly and sincerely interested to the point of excitement in what we are doing, we remove restrictions which otherwise hamper our potentials. Our capacities drive forward with a tremendous surge of inner power. Enthusiasm gives vitality to ability. It reinforces our talents with zest and energy; it adds a magnetic attractiveness. An architect once built a model of a beautiful church which he had designed. The model was exquisite in symmetry, line and detail, but something was missing; it was lifeless and cold. Then he placed a light inside and suddenly the inertness was gone. The little church glowed with warmth and life and beauty.

Enthusiasm does that to our abilities—it places a light inside. It makes them glow with warmth and vitality. The word itself comes from the root meaning of "god-possessed"; this makes clear both the source and the importance which the ancients attached to the quality of enthusiasm. A glance at its synonyms reveals why this should be so—eagerness, warmth, ardor, fervor, verve, vigor. Nothing kindles fire like fire; when we are aflame with enthusiasm, our powers expand and our wholeheartedness becomes contagious.

But enthusiasm, imagination and even purpose cannot

reach satisfying objectives until they are yoked with persistent, determined effort. It follows, then, that *we must persevere in the use of our talents.*

A man overheard an aged Irishman giving some advice to a boy who was boarding a ship to seek his fortune. "Now, Michael, me boy," the old man said, "just remember the three bones and you'll get along all right." The curiosity of the bystander prompted him to ask the Irishman what he meant by the three bones. "Sure, now," replied the aged son of Erin with a twinkle in his eye, "and wouldn't it be the wishbone, the jawbone, and the backbone? It's the wishbone that keeps you going after things. It's the jawbone that helps you ask the questions that are necessary to finding them, and it's the backbone that keeps you at it until you get them!"

A. J. Cronin, the author, describes an incident [4] which proved to be the turning point in his career. He was a successful doctor in the west end of London. Yet he was dissatisfied and vaguely unsure of himself. He seemed to be searching for something, but he had no idea what it was. In due time he developed indigestion. Consulting a colleague, he found that he had a gastric ulcer and was prescribed six months' complete rest in the country and placed on a milk diet. He went to a little farm in the Scottish Highlands where he soon learned that there is nothing more agonizing to an active man than enforced idleness. After a week of indolence he was almost beside himself. Then an idea struck him suddenly. For years he had wanted to write. "By Heavens!" he said, "this is my opportunity. Gastric ulcer or no gastric ulcer, I'll write a novel!"

He walked to the village and bought two dozen exercise books and some pencils. The next morning he sat down at a table, opened an exercise book and waited for an inspiration. Three hours later, when he was called to lunch, he was still sitting there; not a scratch of writing was on the page before him. After lunch, the writing idea seemed like a silly whim and he almost decided to forget it. Then he recalled the sharp advice of an old schoolmaster on how to write. "Get it down!" the schoolmaster had said. "If it stops in your head it will always be nothing. Get it down!" He went upstairs and started again.

For the next three months he tried to "get it down," but it was agonizing business. He spent hours laboring over a sentence, looking for an adjective, correcting and recorrecting the pages until they looked like a spider's web. Yet as his characters took shape the plot began to haunt him. If an idea struck him in the middle of the night he would light a candle and scribble it down. He gained facility in expressing himself and the task of writing became easier.

When he was halfway through the novel, a sudden desolation gripped him. "Why am I wearing myself out with this toil for which I am unequipped?" he asked himself. "What's the use of it? I ought to be resting." He read the chapters he had written. Never had he seen such nonsense, he thought; no one would read it! Stalking out, he threw the manuscript in the ash can and went for a walk in the drizzling rain.

Down the loch shore he came on old Angus, the farmer, patiently digging in the ditch along his little boggy patch of land. When he told Angus about throwing the manuscript away, the old farmer's keen blue eyes scanned him with a queer contempt. "No doubt you're the one that's right, doctor, and I'm the one that's wrong," he finally said. "But my father ditched this bog all his days and never made a pasture. I've dug it all my days and I've never made a pasture. But pasture or no pasture, I can't help but dig. For my father knew and I know that, if you only dig enough, a pasture can be made here." He turned his back on the doctor and continued with his digging.

Half resentfully, Dr. Cronin realized that the Scots farmer had something he did not have, a terrible stubbornness to see the job through at all costs. A new resolve claimed him

as he tramped back to the house. He rescued the soggy manuscript from the ash can, dried it in the kitchen oven, flung
it on the table and set to work with a ferocious energy. He
would not be beaten! Some weeks later he wrote "finis." He
did not care whether his writing was good, bad or indiffer-
ent; he had finished!

He chose a publisher, mailed the manuscript and promptly
forgot it. Some days later, as he went around the village saying good-bye to his friends, the postmaster handed him a
telegram. It was from the publisher with an urgent invitation
to talk with him about the book. He left the post office and
walked down the loch road until he found John Angus. Without a word he showed him the telegram.

The novel he had thrown into the ash can was *Hatter's
Castle*. It became the book of the month, was dramatized
and serialized, translated into nineteen languages, and purchased by Hollywood. Some three million copies have been
sold. The author's life was changed completely because a
stubborn farmer had challenged him to put all his abilities
to work and to persevere.

Probably most of us never will write a novel, but the principle is the same in whatever endeavor we engage. To find
the happiness which comes through making the most of our
abilities, we must persevere in using them and make them
responsive to our bidding. Persistent effort often spells the
difference between success and failure. As in splitting a log,
in which all former ax strokes are wasted if we do not keep
at it until we strike the last blow, so we waste our energies
unless we demonstrate the tenacity to endure until the walls
of difficulty crumble and our abilities come into their own.
Certainly little of lasting worth ever has been accomplished
except by those who have dared to persist in the face of
frowning circumstances. Something within them was superior to the obstacles they encountered.

A final suggestion is to *fill our present place to overflowing*.

Whatever position we may occupy, we can give it the benefit of our finest effort. A man may say to himself, "I am too good for this job. It is too small a position for a person of my talents. There is no opportunity here to expand my powers." In contempt, he refuses to invest his complete capacities in the meager job. Inevitably he becomes dissatisfied, restless and unhappy. He fails his responsibility; he fails his own future opportunity; and, worst of all, he fails himself.

A successful and greatly revered businessman in a western state says that in his early life his mother gave him a priceless gift, a vision of service. "Arthur," she told him, "it is not how much you can get from a job that is important. It is how much you can put into it that counts." The success and influence which radiate from his kindly life reveal how fully he has followed his vision. In recounting the incident, he said, "Through all the years, I have never forgotten what my mother said that day. I have tried to live by the principle of not how much, but how well."

Talent, like muscle, grows through exercise. If we fail to extend ourselves and merely go through the motions while we wait for something more fitted to our abilities to come along, we are headed for continual frustration. We may think that we have ability enough to warrant starting at the top, but almost the only chance to start at the top is in digging a hole!

Consider this fine sentence: "God has never put anyone in a place too small to grow." Wherever our place may be—on the farm, in the office, behind a counter, at a teacher's desk, in a kitchen, wearing a uniform, or caring for a child—when we fill that place to the best of our abilities, personal growth is inevitable. Three things, at least, begin to happen. We do a better job of what we are doing. We expand our talents through vigorous use. And we fit ourselves for larger responsibility and wider opportunity.

CHAPTER VII

The Art of Living Together

THE art of living together in happy marriage is a difficult achievement, judging from what is happening to American family life. The American divorce rate is the highest in the world. Since 1870, it has increased more than 400 per cent. In 1900, there were 55,751 divorces; in 1930, there were 195,-961, or one divorce in every six marriages; in 1946, there were 610,000 divorces—an all-time high—representing one divorce in every three or four marriages. In 1950, the rate dropped slightly to one divorce in every five marriages. About five thousand foolish marriages are annulled each year. These do not include thousands of separate maintenance decrees and as many unlitigated separations. Such a situation vitally affects the children in these broken homes and to a marked degree colors the public morals and the social welfare of the entire nation.

In spite of such appalling figures, the fundamental trouble is not with marriage itself, but with those who marry. Essentially, the problem of creating a happy home is not to have the right person share it, as important as that is, but to *be* the right person. An objective appraisal of the factors leading to divorce deepens the conviction that the major obstacle confronting a successful marriage is *the emotional immaturity of one or both of the partners in the home.* When a clergyman performs a solemn service to unite a man and woman in marriage, the ceremony does not change their personalities by a subtle spiritual alchemy. They carry their behavior patterns, attitudes and inner tensions with them into the new relationship. Immaturity can throw an almost intolerable strain on marriage, causing resentment, heart- ache, hatred, vicious retaliation and broken homes.

One of the chief marks of immaturity is *selfishness,* a pat- tern carried over from childhood. Every child starts out in life as a selfish egotist; the world pivots around him. He thinks of existence in terms of what he can get out of it to gratify his hungers and desires. As he matures, an ever- radiating circle of interests expands his horizons and takes him outside himself. But the emotionally immature stop at varying levels in the growing process. Adult in body and mind, they still demand that the world's orbit circle around them—their comforts, their satisfactions, their whims and their pre-eminence. They consider each situation in relation to what they get out of it. Carried over into marriage, such immaturity causes havoc. After her divorce, a woman wrote: "If my husband had given me the beating I deserved when I threw a tantrum to get my own way, this divorce never would have happened." She was overstating—her remark is not to be interpreted as an argument in favor of wife-beating —but it is important to note the immature pattern of be- havior that she had carried into adult life. As a child she had learned that when she cried, usually she got her own way. If tears did not work, she would exhibit a tantrum to gain her objective. It worked when she was three, it still worked when she was thirteen, it had become an established be- havior pattern long before her marriage at twenty-three. If her husband crossed her wishes or thwarted her desires, she went into a tantrum to force his submission. Finally he de- cided to stand it no longer.

The woman may expect her husband to place her on a pedestal, to play up to her temperament, to toady to her whims, and to grant her luxury, flattery and security. She considers it her right to have whatever her friends may possess—fine clothes, money, an imposing home, social standing. At the same time, she may resent her husband's business or profession; it demands time and attention that could be used to satisfy her personal desires, in impressing her associates, or in climbing the social ladder. Probably she dislikes and mistrusts her husband's friends, except those whom she chooses. That she has obligations to the marital relationship seldom occurs to her. Often she is fearful and selfish in the physical relations with her husband, far more concerned with her own aesthetic reactions than in finding the fulfillment of love, the welding of two happy lives and the creation of the family, as God intended sex to do.

Men can be equally immature. A husband may consider his home a service station, to all intents and purposes. He expects his wife to begin pampering him where his mother left off. She is to share his prejudices, agree with his views on economics and politics, like his friends and ignore her own, take charge of the rearing of their children, including their spiritual training, and give him affection, sympathy and understanding in all his moods. She may know almost nothing about her husband's business or the problems he faces; he does not consider it important that she should. He demands perfection in his wife and, when she cannot live up to the impossible standard he sets, he becomes intolerant, critical and sarcastic. He assumes that his chief responsibility in marriage is to provide his wife with material comfort; she becomes the sleek and expensive symbol of his worldly success. In a modern novel,[1] a disillusioned wife says, "That's what he marries for—a home; a pitch of his own; a place to bring his things to and wherein to keep his things . . . a place where he can have his wife and his children and his dogs and his books and his servants and his treasures and his slippers and his ease, and can feel, comfortably, that she and they and it are his." It fails to occur to the man that his wife has emotional, intellectual and spiritual needs that no amount of possessions can satisfy. When she is unhappy, he is amazed. "Haven't I given you everything?" he demands.

He may seek to possess the personality of his wife completely. He demands her entire attention; he absorbs her total energies. He strives to make her dependent on him and to dominate her will. "He says he loves me deeply and that I mean more to him than anything else in the world," said a wife with desperation in her eyes. "But he really doesn't love *me*, because he can't stand the things I am when I'm truly myself. He loves the things I'm not, which I act out because I know it pleases him." Her husband would have declared in all sincerity that he adored his wife and that she was perfect for him in every way; he would have been horror-struck that she questioned the genuineness of his emotion. Yet she was right. What her husband loved, in a strange possessiveness, was a projection—an ideal of what he thought a wife should be, an image which she sensed and struggled desperately to fulfill. When from time to time she attempted to throw off the artificial role, she met such coldness and hostility in her husband that she made the effort less and less frequently. But the more she conformed to the pattern which her husband demanded, the deeper grew her inner desperation. Immature possessiveness, in whatever form it takes, causes intense unhappiness.

The truth is that both have entered into marriage in the wrong spirit; both are selfish and immature. The real meaning of love lies not in what it can gain, but in what it can impart. Love finds more satisfaction in the joy it bestows than in the delight it receives. It is possible to give without loving, but it is impossible to love without giving. Because it is completely unselfish, mature love begets love. "If you wish to be loved," counseled wise Benjamin Franklin, "be lovable."

There is small mystery about falling in love. Perhaps that is part of the trouble. Love consists of infinitely more than an ecstatic infatuation. Mere physical attraction, or to become enamored with one or two characteristics, is a dangerously narrow foundation on which to build a lasting marriage. The characteristics may change, the physical attraction may wane (it is sure to do so unless supported by intellectual and emotional affinities), and love diminishes into a vacuum of boredom and antipathy. Stephen Leacock wrote, "Many a man who has fallen in love with a dimple has made the mistake of marrying the whole girl."

A cultured Oriental, asked the difference between marriage in America and in his country, replied thoughtfully, "In China, marriage is like a cool teakettle on a hot stove; after a time it comes to a boil. Here, it is like a hot teakettle on a cold stove. After a time it cools off." Without debating the merits of the two systems his comparison suggests, there can be no doubt that a lasting love cannot endure on superficial attraction. Lack of common purposes, ideals and desires places an almost intolerable strain on the marriage tie. Mutual respect is no less important. No matter how attractive a man may be to a woman, love between them will fade unless he can win and maintain her respect. Regardless of how deeply a woman may appeal to a man, his emotion will change if he cannot admire and respect her.

The art of living together demands a realistic view of marriage, not some hopelessly romantic fairy-tale attitude. In fairy stories, the prince and the princess get married and "live happily ever after"—but that is only in storybooks. In real life, the prince soon discovers that his idol has feet of clay. She is afraid of mice, insects, snakes and thunderstorms, and she will not set foot in a dark hallway. She is gay one day and moody the next, for no explainable reason—and then she simmers with resentment. When he asks her why, she answers "Because." In handling the household budget, she fails to exemplify the faith set forth once and for all by his mother—and she backslides tragically, too, as a pastry cook. She is sensitive about trifles; her feelings are hurt when he overlooks her birthday, does not kiss her good night, or fails to compliment her on a nice meal. She chatters the neighborhood gossip when he wants to read the newspaper, yet she turns on the television when he talks about the office. He never realized she would look like that without her make-up and with her hair in curlers, either!

For her part, the princess finds that her prince falls decidedly short of perfection. He has an amazing bump of egotism and likes to feel that he is important, yet he does not seem to know how to put his best foot forward, or to make himself appreciated—by his boss, for instance. He is not observing, does not seem to interpret her moods or desires, and is slow to praise her, no matter how hard she may strive to win his approval. He has a knack at scattering things around the house, is grouchy when he gets up in the morning, looks terrible until after he shaves, and the way he handles his knife and fork is atrocious. As a lover he is far too insensitive and direct. He seems to take her for granted, but he likes to be pampered and is susceptible to flattery—especially from another woman. He brings guests home without warning her in advance, and his salary is nothing like the amount of money her father used to make.

Once they have cleared some of the star dust from their eyes, they can get down to the interesting business of living. The romantic visions they lose are not as important as the realities they discover. Since neither is perfect, they can apply their heads and their hearts to the problems of adjustment, viewing each other clearly for the first time, as it were, and finding much to love in what they see. As they accept each other's peculiarities, they begin a growth which can continue throughout a lifetime filled with tang and happiness. If they will approach their mutual problems with common sense and unselfishness, if they determine not to stand on their rights or to retain their idealistic notions of perfect bliss, if they go "all out" to make their marriage work, they will succeed in building a happy home, rich in satisfactions and companionship.

It is common knowledge that love is stronger than death. Men have laid down their lives for their families, mothers for their children, and children for their parents. On doomed ships, men have stepped back to give their places in a lifeboat to others. Love is stronger than death, but this is not as remarkable as the fact that love is stronger than life, as Channing Pollock has pointed out. Life can become trivial and sordid. It makes enormous demands—poverty, illness, change, frustration and decay. Mundane duties and bitter defeats swallow its joys. Dreams die, worries haunt us, friends fail us and children cause us grief. Yet through it all, undaunted, a realistic love takes rootage, grows and flowers. "Love suffereth long, and is kind . . . beareth all things, believeth all things, hopeth all things, endureth all things. Love never faileth." But first marriage must outgrow its sentimental romanticism.

Love must be fed. In a truly happy home, it feeds on *appreciation*. Wings are added to marriage simply by expression of the gratitude that each of the partners actually feels. As a rule, it is not the big, bad things which wrench a marriage apart; it is the nice little things which are overlooked or forgotten. Married couples are bound by golden threads of precious experience, but habit dulls the eyes. If the news were broadcast that in five minutes an atomic attack would blow our city into oblivion, we would clog the telephone lines with our frantic efforts to tell someone of our love. Why do we wait for an emergency? Too often we resemble the Vermont farmer who was sitting with his wife one evening, looking at the beautiful valley before them. The descending sun laid long friendly fingers of shadow across the fields, and the scene was filled with peace. At last the farmer spoke quietly, as if reluctant to break the spell. "Sarah," he said, "we've had a lot of ups and downs together during these forty years, and when I've thought of all you've meant to me, sometimes it's been almost more than I could do to keep from telling you!"

Your husband is dependable and loyal. He is thoughtful in many ways. True, he is no Adonis and he has his failings, but you love him in spite of his faults. It will help to tell him so. Why not say to him more frequently, especially after some minor success, "I'm proud of you"? Instead of cataloging his faults—all men have them—it may enlarge your sense of appreciation to count the virtues which fall on the credit side of the ledger. We can think appreciation, or we can think criticism; the attitude we assume goes far in shaping the success of marriage. A negative, critical attitude, sowing dragon's teeth, will harvest an ever-growing number of ills to criticize. A friendly, appreciative attitude will help to produce the positive qualities we most admire. But it is necessary to express the gratitude we feel. A woman said, "I never compliment my husband, and I never pass on a compliment that I have heard about him from another. I am afraid he will get conceited." Although it is true that some men have such sensitive bodies that when patted on the back their head swells, a wife runs a greater risk in not doing so; someone else may. In love she wisely looks for his admirable characteristics and builds them through appreciation. If she compliments the good qualities, later there will be fewer bad ones to criticize. Most of us work best in the sunshine of approval.

Gratitude is not a one-way street, however. A husband does well to remember the loving and thoughtful things his wife does daily for the welfare of the family and for his personal comfort. One of the basic drives in human nature is the desire to be appreciated. To feel "taken for granted" is almost fatal to marriage. When Teddy Roosevelt ran for the presidency on the Bull Moose ticket and was defeated, he wired to his wife, "You will see by the newspapers that I am defeated, but nothing matters to me so long as I have you and the children." One can imagine how Mrs. Roosevelt felt when she received the message. Such tender words add strands to the unseen cable which binds a home together. But must we wait until after defeat or disaster to send a telegram filled with tenderness?

The *feeling* of appreciation is important, also. Reasons for gratitude always are present, but unhappiness can creep into the home because we fail to sense them. By putting on spectacles of gratitude, we learn to appreciate what we have instead of making ourselves miserable with what we have not. A couple became dissatisfied with their home and put it in the hands of a real estate agent. Not long after, an advertisement seemed to describe the house of their dreams. They called the agent to discover that the dream house was their own! They failed to appreciate what they had until they read a description of it written by an outsider. If we take a fresh look at what we have, a new sense of gratitude may lift our love and brighten our marriage.

In flying across the Atlantic, one gets used to the drone of the motors. They fall into the background of consciousness; they become a part of the environment. But let an engine sputter and quit, and every passenger is tense and alert. Marriage is something like that; as long as everything runs smoothly, we tend to take it for granted. A husband comes home in the evening and his wife is there. He kisses her perfunctorily, settles into an easy chair and hides behind a newspaper. He eats dinner with his thoughts elsewhere and answers her attempts at conversation in monosyllables. It fails to occur to him to thank her for the meal. He resembles the man whose wife invited a word of appreciation for a carefully prepared dinner by asking, "Was the food all right?"

"Of course it was all right," snapped her husband. "If there had been anything wrong with it, I would have told you."

But once the motor misses and she *isn't* there, how alert he becomes. She is ill, or out of town, or there has been a disagreement that morning and the house is empty when he returns. An hour passes—two—three. The house grows enormous with silence. The radio reports a bus accident in which several people were injured. His imagination runs rampant. Then a familiar step sounds in the hall and a cheery voice calls, "Hello!" He hides his relief and growls, "Where have you been all evening?" But for a few days he is conscious that she is around the house! Perhaps the motor should miss more often just to shake him awake and make him alert to his blessings.

Love is a sensitive plant, but it grows sturdy under careful cultivation. When pressures rise, they should press the partners in the home more closely together; sustaining each other, they find resources to meet them. When reverses struck, a man said, "I don't mind this so much for myself, but I hate to have Mary go through it. She doesn't deserve it. You know, Dominie, she's a fine person!" Later his wife confided, "I'm not bothered too much by what has happened; I know that I can manage. But I'm worried about John. He's taking it like a brick, but he's working too hard to get back on his feet. You know, there just aren't many men like John!" Something deep and tender thrives when we refuse to take each other for granted.

Love is fed also by *understanding.* Understanding encompasses a concern for the fundamental needs, hungers and dreams of the mate in our home. We learn that there are basic differences in the way a man and a woman think and act, and to respect the differences. For instance, a man considers himself unselfish when he avoids giving trouble *to* others; a woman thinks of unselfishness as taking trouble *for* others. Not knowing this, each will regard the other as basically selfish. A woman is more devious in her thinking than a man, to the male's constant bewilderment. If they arrive at the same conclusions, invariably it is by different routes; as a rule the woman's intuitive guess is as correct as the man's reasoned certainty.

At a dinner party, apropos of the conversation in progress, a man stated bluntly, "This talk about women's intelligence is foolish. There isn't a woman alive who wouldn't rather be beautiful than clever."

"Quite true," answered the woman at his right, "and the reason is that so many men are stupid and so few are blind!"

A husband should not be so stupid, though, as to fail to realize the part that love plays in a wife's life. A man's heart embraces the world; a woman's world centers in the heart. Love is essential to her; that is why she married in the first place. In part, her desire may have been for security and a home, but deeper still it was for love and companionship. A man never wins the woman he loves by promising, "Darling, marry me and I'll pay the bills, provide for your old age, trim the lawn and even wash the dishes occasionally!" What he says is, "Darling, I'm crazy about you! I adore you! I can't live without you!" She believes him because this is what she wants to hear. It comes as a shock when after the honeymoon her husband seems more concerned with his business than in holding her in his arms, or more interested in cultivating his hobby than in her recital of the day's happenings. He even forgets to pet her and to tell her that he loves her. This explains in part why a woman becomes a bridge fanatic, a society climber, or pours out her love on her children until it becomes a possessive and abnormal "smother" love.

To a woman, love is an emotional state. She is so constituted that it cannot be otherwise. She cannot reconcile herself successfully to love as a *fait accompli* between two people who have blended their lives intimately and inseparably. Love remains for her a dynamic, demonstrative thing; she desires continuing evidences of concern and affection. Many husbands would create deeper happiness if they spent less effort in achieving material success and gave more attention to the little, companionable, loving acts which weave married lives together.

A clergyman selected an exotic negligee and instructed the clerk, "Send it to my wife. I am the Reverend Mr. Blank," and gave the address. The clerk's head came up with surprise and her eyes opened wide as she asked, "Are you a minister?" With a smile he admitted that he was. "I've heard of men who seem to think that other pastures are greener," he told her, "but I think it is wiser to spend time in cultivating my own!"

An unexpected gift, some flowers, a telephone call, a love note left on the dressing table where it is easily found, a well-merited word of appreciation, a compliment on her new hair styling or her chic dress, a grateful remark that starts, "One of the things I like about you, dear, is . . ."—all such acts are small and take little time, but they smooth many heartaches and repay much sacrifice, for they are made great by a woman's gratitude. Basically and above all, every wife wants her husband to esteem and cherish her, and longs for him to make his love vivid.

There is another side to the picture, of course. A woman, too, can grow complacent after marriage; subconsciously she may take the attitude, "I'm wed now, so I can let down a little." Before she is aware of it, the little becomes a lot— enough, at least, to steal her attractiveness and to irritate her husband. She may become careless about her home or her personal appearance, she may neglect to prepare meals or to wash dishes, she may fail to take the interest in her husband and in his work that she did before they were married. She may allow herself to fall into picayune habits that annoy her husband and, although she knows that they trouble him, makes no effort to correct them. A girl, well-groomed and attractive before her marriage, lazily let her personal appearance slip. She became casual to the point of indifference about her husband's idiosyncrasies, one of which was promptness for appointments, a fact which she had respected before their marriage. One day, after constantly growing tension, her husband walked out of the home, avowing his intention not to return. She was genuinely bewildered. "I love Jim," she sobbed to her pastor. "I would do anything for him."

"Literally anything?" he inquired.

"Yes, literally anything."

"Would you go to the point of keeping yourself well-groomed, to take advantage of being the attractive woman that you are, and to be punctual with your meals and appointments?"

She raised thoughtful eyes. "Do you mean that those are really the reasons that Jim walked out? I thought . . ."

"Jim has talked with you about these things, hasn't he? They may seem small to you, but are they more than your husband has a right to expect? Jim loves you and wants to feel proud of you. Your tardiness, since you knew that it annoyed him, became a symbol of what he considered your callous disregard of his desires and sensibilities."

It was not difficult to make Jim see how impulsive his action had been, and, since Joan did a thorough about-face as her part of the bargain, the story had a happy ending. Not all marital rifts are healed as easily as this, but it serves to illustrate that thoughtless trivialities can strain marriage to the breaking point.

Love is fed by appreciation, understanding—*and something more*. Love must be kept a vibrant, living, growing thing; it must not fall into dull routine or boredom. Growth infers change. The man or the woman we married three years, or five years, or twelve years ago is not the same person to whom we are married today. Time refuses to stand still. But each chapter of change can add piquancy and joy. For love in marriage is friendship raised to the highest key. It is the willingness to accept each other as we are, not as a projection of our own desires or as a mirror before which to preen our egotisms, not as someone to make over or a means to an end, not a perfect being, but simply a part of humanity like ourselves, with the same weaknesses, foibles and irrationalities, the same strengths, virtues and admirable qualities—only with something unique which makes each of us what we are; someone, in short, whom we can love simply for himself and for what we see in him. This kind of friendship has tensile strength; it will not snap when the weight is heavy, or the pull is long. It has resiliency and bounces back when thrown down hard. It has longevity—it lasts. The earlier wildly leaping flame has steadied into a constant glow that warms our hearts and softens our features when we glance at each other. It is affection, admiration and esteem. It is sharing—the sharing of joys and laughter, and tears and heartaches, and burdens bravely borne, and monotony taken in stride. It is sacrifice without whimpering, and words without malice when they could cut like a knife. It is the need for each other, and tenderness, and dreams like banners, and minor victories magnified by love into major triumphs. It grows deeper with the passage of the years.

Because it is a growing thing, there must be room for differences and disagreements. Marriages would grow dull indeed if the individuality of one of the partners grayed down to a drab neutral, or became a weak reflection of what the other thought and did. If a man says, as happens on rare intervals, "My wife and I have lived together for thirty years, and we've never had an argument or a cross word," either he is not telling the truth or he is a nincompoop! Such lack of spirit may be admirable in a sheep, but not in a human. Is it possible to imagine anything more boring than to be caged in a situation not vibrant enough to generate even a lively difference of opinion? Action and reaction are attributes of life; without them an object is dead—including a marriage! One of the attractive forces, in the first place, was that intangible quality called personality, and a personality without spirit is as insipid as soup without salt. Where there is spirit there will be sparks. The fact that they fly occasionally adds zest to marriage.

It also aids mental health. Some couples, taught that it is wrong to express themselves forcibly, or under the impression that marital harmony demands the suppression of anger and resentment, bottle such emotions inside and turn bland countenances to each other. They do not realize that these emotions, with others such as hostility, fear, vanity and ambition, are as normal as feelings of tenderness, love and devotion. If not given release, they will break out later in ill health or resentful acts which neither can understand. Suppressed emotions store up dynamite which some stray marital short circuit may explode disastrously. If there are hurt feelings or misunderstandings in the home, it is wise to get them in the open in order to deal with them sensibly. Often to express a resentment in words—or action—is to destroy it.

A certain couple have made an outstanding success of their marriage, although both are strongly temperamental. Early in their marriage, the husband became angry and smashed a plate. His wife smashed a second plate immediately. He broke another and she matched it. By the time they reached the sixth plate, the humor of the situation struck them and they started to laugh. They laughed until they cried, holding each other in their arms. "It cost more money than we could afford," the wife explained, "but it was worth it. We learned a lesson. Whenever he'd lose his temper, I'd hand him the nearest plate—or he would do the same to me—and that was the end of it!"

Possibly to break dishes is not the best method of marital adjustment, but each couple can work out a technique to help keep their emotional balance. Talking it out usually is sufficient. It is healthy for a man to say to his wife, if he feels it keenly, "Dear, your brother Bill is a pain in the neck," and for the wife to return with equal candor, "Your Aunt Emma is no bargain, either. And what's more, I don't like the way you go around spilling ashes on the rug." Such a prelude can lead to a productive marital spat, productive because it gets ill-will into the open, lets off emotional steam and acts as a safety valve; and productive also in revealing how strong their relationship is and how deeply they love each other. If a couple holds mutual respect, admiration and love, joined with a saving sense of humor, they need not fear an occasional quarrel. Facing their hostilities honestly and openly helps to stabilize their marriage.

This does not imply the right to say every caustic or hurtful thing which comes to mind. An angry word has a cutting edge; it inflicts a wound which may not heal easily. Ugly accusations breed bitterness. We cannot give vent to our emotions without restraint and expect our mates to forget all that is said in vindictiveness or anger. Most marital graves are not opened all at once, but by a series of little digs. Some words are better unsaid. In fact, one of the rules of successful marriage is to refrain each day from uttering three uncomplimentary or critical things which we are tempted to say.

In numerous instances thus far we have referred to marriage as a partnership, and so it is. One of life's cardinal laws is that the world is made up of pairs, and marriage is no exception. Each component in the pair supplements and compliments the other. We have two eyes; they are not rivals, but partners. We have two ears; they serve in harmony. We have two hands; each strengthens the work of the other. There are two sexes; each fortifies and fulfills the other. Marriage at its finest is a partnership in which each supplements and completes the other. Gordon Higman wrote:

Woman was not taken from man's head to be ruled by him,
Nor from his feet to be trampled upon,
But from his side to walk beside him,
From under his arm to be protected by him,
And from near his heart to be loved by him.

The first essential in establishing a partnership is the care with which we select the person with whom we form it. This is the foundation on which either a good business or a successful marriage is built. Like any partnership, it requires certain qualities to make it successful, such as honesty, loyalty, kindness and faith. Both must be motivated by a sincere desire for fair play, a willingness to accept the setbacks as well as the successes, and a determination to make the partnership work regardless of the conditions encountered.

Thus they become one—one in intent, purpose, loyalty and love. In marriage as in business most problems can be solved if each partner assumes a just responsibility in the enterprise and is as quick to serve as to benefit. Married happiness is simply the golden rule applied at close quarters. It is an art; indeed, "the greatest of all arts is the art of living together," William Lyon Phelps maintains.

A happy marriage is marked by a sense of equality and mutual consideration. It is not an arena for a constant contention of wills, a covert struggle for superiority. There is enough tyranny in the world without admitting it to the home, enough dictators without having them rule from the kitchen, at the head of the table—or from the nursery! Then the wedded ideal becomes an ordeal. Mutual respect, trust, love and consideration are the keynotes, together with the readiness for each to carry a full share of the load. "The marriage carriage must be pulled by a team; it isn't a one-horse shay," someone has written. Or, to change the figure, marriage should resemble the bicycle built for two. Sometimes grandfather sat in front and guided the vehicle, and sometimes grandmother did. Each knew that the other was there, and each undertook to co-operate. Neither dragged his feet nor let the other do all the work; both pedaled in unison. Both kept a sense of balance and, when they arrived, they arrived together. This democratic spirit of co-operation and fair play did not go out of style with the two-seated bicycle! When a man and a woman are welded in a true partnership, they are prepared to meet the exacting problems which every home must face.

One is the economic hurdle, the problem of making both ends meet. The strain in doing so is aggravated by the fact that other couples have comforts and conveniences denied to them. Perhaps the wife has had her own income before marriage. Possibly she earned more than her husband does now and she feels financially cramped. Irritations arise. The husband interprets them as criticism of his lack of earning power. The wife feels at least an implied criticism on her ability to economize in handling the family budget. The man may seek to control expenditures and become niggardly in the amount of money he gives his wife. One such wife, tired of daily budget battles with a stingy husband, finally inquired wearily, "When I took the marriage vows, by any chance did you understand me to say love, honor and *no pay?*"

It would come as a shock to some men to realize that one third of the wage earners in the nation are women, many of them heads of families. The day is past when women are ignorant in financial matters. They must be treated as intelligent adults in the use of the family income if marriage is to know any high degree of happiness.

Nor is a husband correct in assuming that, because he brings home the pay envelope, it is *his* money. Insurance counselors have pointed out that, if he were to pay for all the work that his wife does in the home, he would have to earn about twenty thousand dollars annually before he could afford to do so. If he makes five thousand dollars or less, the wife is contributing more than he is to the home—just by managing the house, doing her own work and caring for the children.

But partnership in the home never can be put on a dollar-and-cents basis. When the spirit of odious comparison comes in the door, love flies out the window. True love gives freely, not in a bargaining mood, or with an eye on the cash register. The family that works as a team can face the most deplorable economic situation and still stay together.

There is no easy answer to the economic strains that beset a household. The situation calls for a mutual sharing, forbearance and understanding. The partners in the home have taken each other "for better or for worse"; if they stand together steadfastly in the worst, they will be together to enjoy the best. Perhaps, after consultation with a qualified person, they should set up a realistic budget. A weekly or monthly financial council, in which the entire family shares, may aid. In any event, a sense of fair play and equality are of great importance. If a woman says, "Look what he gives me to run the household, but see what he spends on his bowling!" or a man complains, "I can't buy a new tool for my work bench without bickering, but I notice that her kitchen is equipped with every convenience," a sense of honest consideration has vanished. It must be re-established if the partnership is to function properly. Likewise, to accept simplicity and frugality not out of grudging necessity, but as a positive ideal, will do much to remove the irritations which arise from limited income. The partners in the home should learn that money cannot purchase the most precious commodities of life, and that they can claim their share of the fundamental joys without it. When sacrifices are accepted as a challenge and in the spirit of love, they can knit two hearts together in a satisfying quality of happiness denied to those who refuse to submit to such discipline.

Two sisters married handsome men. One husband was from a wealthy family and in a short time inherited a large amount of money. The marriage was marked by bitter arguments and separations, and finally ended in divorce. The other husband was struggling to gain a foothold in his profession. In commenting on her sister's unhappy marriage, his wife said, "I believe the trouble was that Virginia and John had it too easy. They didn't have to struggle for anything and so they drifted apart. Tom and I have been so busy fighting the world that we haven't had time to fight each other."

No one can maintain with any seriousness that grinding poverty, filled with tensions and anxieties, is good for marriage. It is true, however, that a happy marriage does not depend on lack of problems, but rather on inner resources sufficient to master them. Those who undergo no disciplines or who face few problems are not to be envied. The emotion of love is not self-perpetuating. Love and nothing else is likely to become nothing else. It endures and grows through exercise in the business of living; testings produce triumphs, and struggles call forth strength. It is literally true that some marriages are successful because they have not had the economic advantages that others have had.

Another problem confronting the married partners is the physical expression of marital love. Sexual maladjustment is one of the major reasons for unhappiness in marriage. Physical attraction and its fullest intimate expression can draw a husband and wife together as few forces can; it is the most complete expression of love and is as old as the human race. The urge for sexual fulfillment is inherent in all mature persons, and an intelligent understanding of the part that sex plays in marriage is basic to a happy home. One of the instinctive outreaches of love is a desire for fusion with the beloved. Fusion, a sense of affinity and completion for two personalities as they meet and flow into each other, takes place on various levels—social, intellectual, emotional and physical. All must be present in a true mating of personalities to produce a supremely happy marriage. But, in a fundamental sense, the physical becomes the symbol and capstone of the others, as the poet Shelley explained in a thought-provoking definition of love: "That profound and complicated sentiment which we call love is the universal thirst for communion not merely of the senses, but of our whole nature. . . . The sexual impulse, which is only one, and often a small part of those claims, serves, from its obvious and external nature, as a kind of type of expression for the rest, a common basis, an acknowledged and visible link."

A feeling of disunity pervades each human being until united in the completeness of love. This can be achieved with comparative satisfaction on the social and intellectual levels, or it can be approached through sublimation; an unmarried woman, for instance, can sublimate her love of children in the nursing, teaching or social service professions, which give outlet for her love. But such attempts at fusion lie under the shadow of incompleteness. In the final analysis, man and woman are made for each other and are not complete until they absorb each other in requited love. This sense of dichotomy was known to Plato, for in his *Symposium* he tells this legend to explain it:

". . . for the original human nature was not like the present, but different. The sexes were not two as they are now, but originally three in number; there was man, woman, and the union of the two, having a name corresponding to the double nature. . . . The primeval man . . . had four hands and four feet, one head with two faces . . . also four ears, two privy members, and the rest to correspond."

They were so strong and mighty in thought that they made an attack on the gods, after which Zeus, who was reluctant to exterminate them, "cut men in two, like a sorb-apple which is halved for pickling, or as you might divide an egg with a hair. . . . After the division of the two parts of man, each desiring his other half, came together, and throwing their arms about one another, entwined in mutual embraces, longing to grow into one. . . ."[2]

The Scriptures speak more succinctly: "Therefore shall a man leave his father and his mother, and shall cleave unto his wife: and they shall be *one flesh*." To complete this fusion, divinely implanted, becomes both the object and the highest attainment of love.

The emotional tone to sexual development begins in infancy and, unfortunately, often is distorted into something shameful and unnatural. It becomes associated with a sense of guilt or uncleanness, often because of the unfortunate attitude of parents, or because of their embarrassment or clumsiness in answering a child's questions, queries which are natural for a child. Perhaps he gets punished for asking them; perhaps, by their evasions, he interprets sex as something nasty or obscene instead of a noble expression of love and parenthood. Perhaps he gets the impression that, even if his parents actually do not punish him, God will. A professional man, poised, substantial and successful, breaks down in the minister's study and admits the hell of agony which he has endured for years because of sexual impotency. His wife had shown amazing understanding and forbearance; that made it possible for him to endure it. When traced to its source with the aid of a psychiatrist, the impotency was discovered to spring from a sense of guilt impressed on a growing boy by stern and impeccable parents who governed themselves and their children by a rigid religious code centering in the "fear" of God. A woman involved in serious marital trouble shudders as she says, "All men are beasts. I should have known; my mother told me so when I was a girl. She said never to let a man touch me, that all any man wanted was my body." Inquiry revealed that, so far as she remembered, her mother and father never showed warmth or affection to each other; in fact, they had quarreled violently and had separated when she was a child. Small wonder that under such distorted emphasis, the physical aspect of marriage should seem a vicious and degraded thing.

It is possible to trace the source of much of the warped spiritual emphasis which at best interprets the physical expression in marriage as a concession to carnal human nature. Some religious attitudes seem to infer that God should have seen fit to provide a better method for procreating the race! Early Judaism recognized marriage and the physical expression of love as honorable, clean and good. "Then the Lord God said, It is not good that the man should be alone; I will make him a helper fit for him." But before the coming of Jesus an Oriental philosophy crept over the Greco-Roman world which said that all material things were carnal and unholy, especially the body and its hungers. Its teachings influenced the primitive Christian Church and the Apostle Paul seems to have been touched by it; marriage, he infers, is a compromise with the flesh. At first the Church battled vigorously against the philosophy that the flesh was vile, but in the fourth century the heresy, strengthened by the impulse toward asceticism, emerged victorious; the physical attraction of man and woman was considered the root of evil superior to that of the love of money. Through the centuries this view has continued in various forms, with resultant untold misery, unhappiness, repression and shame.

Today, enlightened religious thinking takes a different viewpoint. It recognizes that marriage is, as God intended it to be from the beginning, a natural, honorable, creative part of life. The Creator formed male and female and saw that what He had made was good, however man might attempt to pervert His intention. "What therefore God hath joined together, let not man put asunder." Marriage nurtures the noblest potentials in human nature; it provides the climate in which they can grow most readily and develop most fully. Physical attractions, according to the Committee on Marriage and Divorce of the National Council of Churches, "have their source in the thought and purpose of God, first for the creation of human life, but also as a manifestation of divine concern for the happiness of those who have so fully merged their lives."

So, according to the religious insight, the physical relationship in marriage should be lifted to the level of beauty and reverence. Common sense and sincere esteem lead to the same conclusion. But such high rewards are not achieved by accident or instinct; married love is a creative enterprise. It can be achieved only if wedded partners, in love and humility, are willing to adventure together with patience and understanding. They should prepare intelligently for this sacred aspect of marriage. They may find it wise to talk to a doctor or marriage counselor competent to deal with such matters. They can read some of the many fine books readily available. They can talk quietly together, facing their difficulties honestly and with the readiness to adjust. If the emotional coloring of their reactions to the sexual act is deep and warped, they will do well to place themselves in the hands of a psychiatrist. In the end, the conquest of difficulties and the consummation of love will make the struggle supremely worth while.

Finally, the art of living together receives its strongest and most subtle aid when the partners in the home are united by *the practice of their religious faith*. The home built on firm spiritual foundations experiences a steadiness and a happiness uniquely its own. Robert Louis Stevenson prayed:

Lord, behold our family here assembled. We thank Thee for this place in which we dwell; for the love that unites us; for the peace accorded us this day; for the hope with which we expect the morrow; for the health, the work, the food, and the bright skies that make our lives delightful; for our friends in all parts of the earth, and our friendly helpers in this foreign isle. . . . Give us courage, gaiety, and the quiet mind. Spare to us our friends, soften to us our enemies. Bless us, if it may be, in all our innocent endeavors. If it may not, give us the strength to encounter that which is to come, that we be brave in peril, constant in tribulation, temperate in wrath, and in all changes of fortune and down to the gates of death, loyal and loving one to another. Amen.

Consider the deep and close-knit family ties of love and

reverence which such a prayer makes manifest. Would any home sustained by such intangible strands fall apart, no matter what frustration or grief might strike? Does not such a spirit enrich happiness and crown it with priceless blessing? And is it not worth attaining?

Such a union begins when a man and a woman stand before their God and take lifelong vows of love, honor and duty. It is better if, by their rearing, they are not strangers to the altar before which they stand. It continues as week after week they place themselves under the influence of a loving Power who gives meaning and depth to their love. As they worship together, seeking spiritual guidance for their daily tasks and placing themselves under the influence of spiritual ideals for their home and their treatment of each other, attitudes are molded deep within at the springs of action. When children come into the home, the sanctuary helps to nurture the kind of character which can stand up to the storms that strike in later years. Such simple observances as reading the Scriptures together, family prayers, and grace before meals exert amazing influence in creating the atmosphere of the home. A man visiting a friend chided him for not saying grace at the family meals. "God knows I'm thankful," the husband defended himself. "Yes," replied the visitor gently, "but the children don't."

Such religious observances create a subtle, spiritual influence in the home which in turn gives birth to a quiet, satisfying happiness denied to those who never sense its worth. Habits of worship and devotion, if they were practiced earnestly in the homes across America, would lessen appreciably the family tensions and marital strife which mars the scene today. "Except the Lord build the house," the Psalmist declared, "they labor in vain that build it."

The woman was ill as she wrote the following letter; her husband was blind. Friends admired them both for their courage and their sunny faith. After her death, the letter was found among her possessions and a friend read it to the husband. Later he memorized it until the words lived in his heart.

My dear, dear husband,

I am sorry that I can leave so little to you in material things, but some sweet memories I hope you will always cherish. Our lovely evening chats, our Ninety-first Psalm, our hope of God's healing those dear eyes, and all the blessed simple things that have made life so sweet with you. May these experiences of our lives together warm your heart while you dream on.

Be sure to have faith and trust His loving care. You are so brave! . . . I have tried to make you my example. Your great patience, your love for everyone, your meekness, your allegiance to your Master and your lack of knowledge of your own greatness! . . . I thank God that He gave me to you for these happy, happy years.

You have done much to make me feel that life was worth living. Your noble soul makes me feel that God will bring us together again, for I am sure He brought our lives together here on earth. Perhaps He will let us do His work together in His Kingdom. . . .

Loving you always, my darling,
Your Wife

CHAPTER VIII

Managing Our Moods

ANOTHER important support to personal happiness lies in the control of our moods. Many find this difficult. They admit ruefully that the refrain of a beloved southland spiritual is descriptive of the emotional pattern of their lives:

> Sometimes I'm up, sometimes I'm down,
> O yes, Lord!

Sometimes they are in the heights and often they plunge into the depths. Their moods vary with the weather, the season, the situation, or seemingly for no reason at all. Realistically, we must learn to live with our moods if we are to maintain a measure of stable happiness. We cannot ignore them or run away from them. Is it possible to manage them with any degree of success?

The answer is affirmative. Through an understanding of the nature of our moods and by the application of certain practical principles, it is possible to gain a marked control over our reactions. We need not remain hapless victims of varying moods; we can manage them with distinct success, if we are willing to pay the price.

Moods come from various sources. The weather seems to affect a large number of people. If the day is dark and gloomy, it transmits that spirit to their mood. However, for some individuals, dark days have a reverse effect. Phillips Brooks, the noted divine, refused to compose a sermon on a rainy day; he had learned through experience that the sermon would be negative and pessimistic. On the other hand, a friend revels in gloomy days, for he finds a beauty in them which elevates his spirit. Too much sunshine, he says, makes him feel uneasy and fills him with a mild melancholy.

Moods also seem to be affected by the change of seasons, the variations in vegetation and the emanations from the sun. Some doctors think that diet, especially the amount of calcium in our systems, has something to do with our moods. The psychological effect of color is well known. That music influences mood is common knowledge; mood music is a valued ally in most fields of entertainment, especially television, radio and the cinema.

We may reasonably expect a low mood to grip us after a period of prolonged tension and strain. It is of great assistance to learn to take this fact for granted and refuse to allow a depressing mood to throw us off balance. When we are physically, mentally and emotionally fatigued, we fall easy prey to the dark mood which is likely to pounce on us. I was impressed by this fact in a story related to me by an unusual man.

In 1952, the American Society of Civil Engineers presented a Centennial of Engineering celebration in Chicago. A part of the program was an exhibition of miniature models of various machines constructed from original drawings by Leonardo da Vinci. These models, numbering over sixty in all, ranged from a multiple firing gun and an aerial bomb to a printing press and an excavation machine. Intrigued by the workmanship exhibited in the models, I learned that an Italian scientist, Dr. Roberto A. Guatelli, had constructed them.

Later I had occasion to meet Dr. Guatelli and to learn his story. The son of a Padua professor, at an early age he had become interested in Leonardo and had made a thorough study of his life and accomplishments. Before World War II, although not a Fascist, he was commissioned by Mussolini to reproduce the models from Leonardo's original drawings. He exhibited them with tremendous success in Italy, in the United States and later in Japan.

The war broke out while Dr. Guatelli was still in the Orient. After Italy's defeat, he was thrown into a Japanese prison camp. Months of horror followed. He witnessed a number of the atrocities committed against American prisoners of war. He learned that his models had been destroyed in an American bombing raid. At the end of the war, the victorious American troops liberated him and he became one of the first witnesses to testify against the Japanese in the atrocity trials. Soon afterward the American government flew him to the United States, and the tension and emotional impact of these frightful years took their toll. He suffered an emotional collapse and fell into a mood of deep despair. Everything seemed futile; he wanted to die.

It is pertinent to note that the low mood came after he had undergone severe emotional and physical strain. Such reactions are almost inevitable after we go through a trying period. We should learn to discount what our emotions tell us when we are tired; then our low mood fails to throw us off balance. It is easier to wait with patience, knowing that the pendulum will swing back again.

It proved so for the Italian scientist. During his depressed mood, his wife encouraged him to rebuild the Leonardo models; he still had access to the drawings. It seemed useless effort to him—and where would they get the materials necessary to build the models? They had no money to purchase them. His wife answered that; they tramped the streets and alleys of the city, often late at night when he could not sleep, searching for materials.

He worked feverishly with the scraps thus acquired. For days he would labor almost continuously, unable to sleep, hardly stopping for food. When he ran out of materials, he and his wife would roam the streets until he could continue his toil. After three months of almost ceaseless labor, the models were completed, over sixty in all. His tension broke and he slept in exhaustion. Slowly his health returned and his dark mood disappeared.

When we are in the grip of discouragement, we are wise to refuse to let gloom say the last word. Figuratively, we can tie a knot on the end of our confidence and hold on. Assured that the clouds will lift, we have the patience to wait for the sun to shine. There is reason for hope when the mood is blackest—probably the upswing will start soon.

It is erroneous, however, to think that somber moods come only after emotional strains or crises. Everyone is subject to cycles of depression and elation, of gloom and good cheer. We may think that certain fortunate individuals are not troubled by dark moods. "Jim is always the same," we may remark. "He always is blithe and happy. He never has a blue moment." We are mistaken. The cycle of ups and downs may not be as marked, or Jim may have learned through discipline not to reveal the low trend, but he has low moods, nonetheless. They come to everyone.

Sydney J. Harris, syndicated columnist, reports that nothing seems to account for his moods; they just come. Since he has learned this, he anticipates them and does not let them upset him. He sits them out quietly and thus "cancels the harm they can do." He confesses that sometimes in the depth of a low mood he thinks his writing is so poor that he hopes the editor will throw it in the waste basket. "Actually," he adds, "the columns I knock out when I am feeling bad are often better than the ones I write in a good mood." He concludes that a depressed person cannot judge his own work accurately.[1]

The attitude in which Mr. Harris meets his bleak moods is

based on sound common sense. When we are melancholy, it is impossible for us to evaluate correctly our personal contributions to our loved ones, our work or to society at large. When we learn to anticipate a bad mood and to accept it philosophically when it comes, when during the period of depression we are wise enough to suspend judgment as to the worth of our achievements, we have made sincere practical advance in managing our troublesome moods.

It helps to speed the waiting process when we force ourselves to *assume a fresh viewpoint*. This entails shutting the door of our minds to hopeless and despairing thoughts and deliberately to appropriate a confident, cheerful attitude. This is an extremely difficult assignment for the person who allows himself to be carried away by his depressed moods, but through discipline of emotions and patient practice it can be accomplished. By an act of will it becomes possible to turn our minds away from gloom and to center them elsewhere.

One winter the battery in our car gave me trouble. The voltage regulator would stick open, allowing the battery to discharge its power uselessly. Our negative thoughts resemble that faulty regulator. They drain off emotional energy needlessly until our inner power is depleted. We must correct their disastrous flow before we can recharge our spiritual batteries with hope and power. Then, stimulated by a confident attitude, the forces of faith and good cheer can flow in to replace the discouragement of a gloomy mood.

The answer on how to break the negative circuit and to start our thoughts flowing constructively varies with the personality of each individual. Often a simple expedient is all that is needed. A woman may discover that it helps to reverse the direction of her pessimistic feelings when she buys a new hat, reads a gay book, helps a neighbor or absorbs herself in a hobby. A man I know gets out his fishing gear when his emotional barometer starts to drop. He sorts his tackle, fondling it with loving touch, and repairs any minor damage. The feel of a rod in his hand sends his mind spinning down the path of pleasant memories. In imagination he pits his skill against a swirling trout or a mighty muskie. Soon he is no longer in the city; he is drinking in the beauty of a quiet lake or casting a fly on a sunflecked stream. It takes a black mood indeed to endure through such an evening! A certain woman, when she feels a low mood approaching, asks her husband to baby-sit while she goes out for a leisurely dinner and a pleasant evening. An executive heads for his work bench in the basement, another gives himself to his garden. Any method which can lift our spirits and induce a fresh attitude is an effective one to use.

A companion suggestion is to *act happily*. Our emotions have a tendency to follow our actions. William James originally stated the psychological principle involved: "The physical expression of an emotion deepens the emotion; while the refusal of expression diminishes the emotion." If we are frightened by an unfamiliar sound, for instance, and start to run, the act of running will increase the fear. If we control our fear, walk casually, whistle nonchalantly perhaps (whistling in the dark is good psychology) and stay relaxed until we discover that the noise is inconsequential—a dog trotting behind us, a tree limb creaking in the wind, or a friend approaching—we reduce the emotion of fear by acting unafraid. Similarly, if we give way to a depressed mood, allowing our shoulders to droop and our faces to sag; if we dwell on the dark side of every experience and snap irritably at those who come near us, the black mood is bound to deepen. If, however, we stand straight with our shoulders back, if we force ourselves to look pleasant even though we do not feel cheerful, if we discipline ourselves to speak courteously to others, in time the baleful mood will lessen and a sunnier spirit will replace it. In the midst of a depressed mood, a wise rule to follow is to speak, act and think as cheerfully as possible.

Another method involves the *practical use of affirmation and prayer*. If our prayers have seemed ineffectual in combating our low moods, perhaps we have allowed them to become sporadic or stereotyped and should give them a fresh cutting edge. On awakening in the morning, for example, in the first moments of consciousness, we can begin the day with an affirmation of confidence and hope. Although this may seem trivial, in reality it helps set the emotional tone for the entire day. We may find it helpful to repeat a sentence from the Psalms, such as, "This is the day which the Lord hath made; we will rejoice and be glad in it," or a line from the Doxology, "Praise God, from whom all blessings flow," or words from a favorite hymn—"Spirit of God, descend upon my heart." Dr. Daniel A. Poling, who has wielded tremendous influence on the youth of America, begins his first waking moments with the affirmation, "I believe!" We will discover that the Scriptures are a rich mine of inspiration from which we can select many phrases—"They that wait upon the Lord shall renew their strength"; "Be of good cheer"; "I can do all things through Christ who strengtheneth me"; "God is love." The habit of starting the day with an affirmation of trust and cheer will tend to lift our spiritual horizons and to turn our thoughts outward, away from the chasm of dejection and toward the Source of power.

Perhaps we have had the experience of hearing a tune over the radio in the morning. We thought we promptly forgot it, yet that afternoon or evening we found ourselves humming the tune. The melody which we assumed we had dismissed from our mind had lodged just below the threshold of consciousness. Although we were not aware of its presence, it had colored our thoughts during the intervening hours.

When we make use of positive affirmation the principle is similar. Early in the morning, with our first conscious thought, we affirm a noble sentiment of confidence and trust. It seeps below the level of consciousness where, like dye dropped into a spring, it colors the stream of thought and emotion. Carrying the constructive spirit of assurance and faith, it becomes an ally in defeating our dark mood.

Likewise it helps to set aside moments throughout the day to devote our minds to happy thoughts, reasons for gratitude and rejoicing. Deliberately we lock the gate on gloomy emotions and saunter through a garden of pleasant memories. We recall what grand friends Tom and Harry are and what a generous thing they did for us recently. A grateful prayer follows for such kind friends. We remember what a beautiful picture our little girl made as she played in the yard, the sunlight glinting from her hair, and we offer a heartfelt prayer that the heavenly Father will aid in making us a better parent. It occurs to us that it is a good land in which we dwell; we picture for an instant what it would mean if the privileges we enjoy were wrenched from us, as has happened to millions of people in less favored areas of the world. Our hearts go out in prayerful gratitude and intercession for this bountiful nation. If we practice faithfully this method of thinking happy thoughts, and of linking prayer with gratitude, in due time it will soften the mood of depression. We shall discover that our situation, as trying as it may seem, is filled with hidden reasons for rejoicing.

At night we can continue with our thankful thoughts, disrobing our soul as we undress our body. In the process, we attempt to lay aside our anxieties and our fears, our resentments and our injured feelings, every hopeless and morbid thought, and every weight "which doth so easily beset us." Also, we can ask forgiveness for every wrongdoing, so that our last thoughts before sleep are those of gratitude and joy. Through the hours of the night the seeds of such thoughts take root in the subsoil of the spirit and blossom into kindlier deeds and quickened appreciations. If we practice such a prayer technique until it becomes second nature, it exerts a mighty effect on banishing low moods and replacing them with happier, sunnier attitudes.

Another strategic approach is to *do something constructive and helpful* whenever we are depressed in spirit. If the effort calls for physical activity on our part, so much the better. Such activity turns our thoughts outward, away from our-selves, guarding us from unhealthy self-concern.

During the depression, a man lost his job. He could not find employment, became morose and irritable, and soon was on the verge of a nervous breakdown. A relative who owned a farm invited him for a prolonged visit. At first, enveloped in the darkest indigo, he did little but mope. Gradually, how-ever, he was drawn into the duties of farm life. He started to feed the chickens and gather the eggs; soon he was milk-ing the cows and running the cream separator. Shortly he was working in the fields and eating like the proverbial har-vest hand. At the end of six months he returned to the city completely restored in health and with a different mental and emotional outlook. In due time he found employment and discovered that he handled his new responsibilities with a greater maturity than he had commanded before. Healthy farm life and constructive physical activity had broken the back of his black moods.

Usually it is not necessary, however, to leave the place where we live to find fresh fields of usefulness. Often it takes only a change of attitude, for there are literally dozens of opportunities for service close at hand. When we volunteer our services at church or synagogue, it may astonish us how quickly we are put to work. In the neighborhood a young mother will be grateful if we sit with her children for an evening; an acquaintance will welcome a helping hand; a lonely person will appreciate an afternoon chat. Day nurseries need volunteers, as do the Boy Scout and Girl Scout organizations, the Campfire Girls, societies for the blind and the handicapped, and the Travelers Aid. Overworked nurses in the hospitals would be left free for important nursing assignments if there were more volunteers to assist them.

Once I called on one of the most vibrant and cheerful persons I know, the wife of a prominent doctor. At her home I was told that she was at the hospital. When I found her, she was in the tiny kitchen of the hospital lunchroom, washing dishes! Characteristically, she had taken hold at the point of need. She must have her periods of depression, although no one would surmise the fact; she keeps herself too busy to pay attention to them.

All about us is opportunity to invest our talents in unselfish service, thus turning our emotional energy into constructive channels instead of allowing it to back into a morass of gloomy self-concern. In combating a low mood, there is a distinct personal advantage in finding a constructive service to perform and in giving ourselves to it wholeheartedly.

A final resource is *the expansion of our personal faith*. By observing the reactions of our fellow men, or through even a superficial study of biography, it becomes apparent that strong and purposeful living inevitably is associated with faith in something or someone. Faith is an integrating force which pulls the loose ends of life together. Bernard Shaw once spoke of an experience: "I began to have scruples, to feel obligations, to find that veracity and honor were no longer goody-goody expressions in the mouths of grown-up people, but compelling principles in myself. . . . The change that came to me was the birth in me of moral passion; . . . All the other passions were in me before; but they were idle and aimless. . . . That passion dignified them, gave them conscience and meaning, found them a mob of appetites and organized them into an army of purposes and principles." [2] Wholeness, purpose and inner satisfaction—and thus, indirectly, the preponderance of healthful moods—depend on such integration. Even faith misdirected and ill-used has tremendous power. Dictators, from Genghis Khan and Napoleon to Hitler and Stalin, recognizing this fact have made faith their stock in trade, directing it to their own brutal ends. Thus "the children of this world" often are wiser than "the children of light" in utilizing the inherent power of belief. An explicit faith, affirmatively used, is the "victory that overcometh the world," as the New Testament declares.

But, someone may object, the knowledge that faith is a powerful constructive force does not solve my problem. As much as I may desire to have faith, it is not possible to acquire it by *willing* to have it. One cannot turn faith on or off as one would operate a water spigot.

Such an objection is valid. It is true that we cannot *will* a vigorous faith for ourselves, but it is not necessary to do so. It is not something which we must acquire; it is something we *have*, as we have discussed earlier. The essential is to recognize faith and to direct it toward worthy objectives and satisfying ends. Certainly to call forth a confident spirit of trust when confronting a dark mood is to help defeat it. William James, attesting its power, wrote, "Every sort of energy and endurance, of courage and capacity for handling life's evils, is set free in those who have religious faith." When we replace anxiety, misgiving and despair with attitudes of assurance and hopefulness, confident in life's worthiness and with belief in its possibilities—in short, when we attack a negative mood with a positive faith—we are using the most effectual force available to overthrow our somber moods.

An incident in the life of the prophet Elijah gleams brightly through the centuries to suggest the practicalities of this resource. Jezebel, the wicked queen, had brought idolatry into the land. The altars of the Most High smoked with incense to pagan gods; the temple of the Lord was profaned and its priests murdered. The people worshiped in weird and bloody rites. Elijah thundered denunciations against these evil influences and challenged Baal's priests to a mighty contest to determine the one true God, Jehovah or Baal. High on Mount Carmel the struggle raged for the soul of a nation. Elijah emerged victorious, only to flee into the desert before the vengeful fury of the queen. Worn out physically and depleted emotionally, a negative reaction set in. His despair was so deep that he wanted to die. "It is enough," he sobbed. "Now, O Lord, take away my life; for I am not better than my fathers."

How he was led step by step from his dark and pessimistic mood is a record of amazing spiritual therapy and the resurgence of Elijah's faith. First came the opportunity to renew himself physically through rest and food, then under divine guidance he traveled to a new locality and a change of scenery. There, after cataclysmic happenings, he listened to a "still, small voice"—and for the first time he saw a glimmer of hope. Certain tasks were laid before him, and at last the mood of despair broke and the future became clear. Now the prophet perceived that God had been near him all the time; his former black mood had bandaged his eyes so that he could not see. With fresh insight he understood that he should never have allowed his despairing mood to rob him of his faith.

When a sense of hopelessness engulfs us, it is time to exercise our faith. It becomes a signal for us to light the candle of hope and to keep it bright and burning. We need not remain slaves to our capricious feelings. "They that wait upon the Lord shall renew their strength"; the mood *will* change, the darkness *will* pass. "Trust God, see all, nor be afraid."

CHAPTER IX

Mastering Our Resentments

ONE day a young man came in to see me, boiling with resentment. His superior had reprimanded him sharply for a mistake which he had not made and, tactlessly, had done so in front of a number of other persons in the office. He had given my friend no opportunity to defend himself or to explain that he was not responsible for the error. Fortunately, the incident occurred just before the lunch hour. Hurt and angry, the young man had slammed out of the office and on an impulse had come in to see me.

Feelings of resentment are common to everyone. There is no individual so mature and well-balanced that he never is tormented by this emotion. The modern pressures under which we live, the tensions under which we work, the anxiety and strain which steal our peace of mind tend to set our nerves on edge. Resentments grow rapidly in such emotional climate. Unless we learn to master them, they can disrupt our homes and our friendships, lower our efficiency, antagonize our associates, ruin our serenity and even wreck our health.

The late Fulton Oursler wrote of a woman who faced an operation for ulcers. When the doctor told her that she was afflicted with ulcers, she responded mirthlessly, "Am I glad!" She asked how much the operation would cost and, aware of her husband's financial status, he replied, "Three thousand dollars."

"Splendid!" she exclaimed. "Am I getting back at my husband. That old tightwad wouldn't buy me a fur coat and that is exactly what it would have cost him. He is going to pay for the coat, whether he wants to or not."

"And you are going to pay, too," the doctor reminded her. "The reason you have ulcers is because of the resentment which you have nursed so long against your husband."

In this modern streamlined existence, resentment and hatred are burdens which we cannot afford to carry. When losing altitude in a vicious storm, so I am told, the crew of a cargo airliner sometimes will cast the freight overboard so that the ship will regain altitude and save itself from destruction. If we are to find the buoyancy and power to soar over the obstacles that confront us in everyday existence, it is essential to discard vindictiveness and grudge-bearing. They add dead weight to the human spirit.

Before discussing some methods of dealing with resentment, two incorrect approaches to the problem should receive consideration. The first of these is to *take out our resentments on someone else*. It seems to be human nature to relieve vengeful feelings by directing them at an innocent victim, often a loved one or a subordinate. The business executive exchanges harsh words with his wife across the breakfast table and his secretary suffers for it later in the morning. The bookkeeper expects a raise in salary, fails to receive it and quarrels with the bus driver because he is carried past his stop. Every sales person knows what it means to be on the receiving end of the customer's ire.

Years ago I was the close-up observer of an incident for which, unwittingly, I was responsible. During school days I worked vacation periods in the canteen of a national guard camp. In the canteen, we formed the habit of addressing every noncommissioned soldier as "sergeant." If he were a sergeant, he accepted the rank as a matter of course. If he were a corporal or a private, he did not mind being addressed as sergeant, or protested good-humoredly. One day I was busy arranging stock when I heard a step on the other side of the counter. Without turning, I inquired, "May I serve you, sergeant?" There was a sudden silence; I glanced around to encounter the cold stare of a second lieutenant! In the confusion of the moment, I could think of nothing to say to correct the mistake, so I said nothing.

At that instant, as fate would have it, a private stepped to the counter beside the irate lieutenant. Unfortunately, the private had failed to tuck his black tie inside the blouse under the proper button. The lieutenant's wrathful eye immediately spotted this breach in military dress and he proceeded to lecture the hapless private in scathing words. One would have surmised that to wear a tie under the improper button was a military disgrace second only to treason!

My sympathy went out to the unlucky private, but I could do nothing but listen. My witless error in addressing the self-important lieutenant had wounded his ego. Considering it beneath his dignity to snarl at me, he poured out his ire on the hapless soldier who chanced to appear. His action did not raise him in my esteem or in that of the private! Taking out our resentments on someone else may relieve wounded feelings momentarily, but it does not master the problem.

A second incorrect method is to *bottle our resentments inside.* "Out of sight, out of mind" does not apply when dealing with emotions.

Perhaps people who display their resentments disgust us. They glare and quarrel and shout; they snub others to show their ill will; they make vindictive remarks. We find such behavior boorish and distasteful, so we resolve never to give way to resentment. Or perhaps, early in childhood, we learned that to express our resentments brought punishment, or robbed us of popularity. We discovered that, when we hid our resentments, we were better able to gain our own desires and to win social approval. We had the vindictive feelings, to be sure—no one escapes them—but we pushed them down inside. We were so successful that finally the process became automatic; we did not recognize what we were doing, or even that we felt resentment at all.

Such a strong emotion as resentment, however, cannot be dismissed this easily. Buried deep within, it struggles for release. It disrupts our sense of well-being, impairs our efficiency and blocks our happiness. In time it attacks our health. Physicians have stated that a strong feeling of resentment is as potent as a disease germ in causing illness; it is the chief personality characteristic of individuals troubled with hypertension. This does not infer that resentment is the cause of all high blood pressure and heart ailments. But it underlines the fact that resentment can be a dangerous enemy to physical health and emotional stability.

It is unwise, then, to crowd down our resentments inside, as we would shove soiled clothing into a laundry bag. There are better methods of handling them. One is to *talk them out*. In this modern day, we are accused of talking too much and of remaining silent too seldom. Lord Cockburn once wrote: "Macaulay suffers from the vice of over-talking and consequently of under-listening." Many suffer from a similar vice. Yet, queerly enough, we often remain inarticulate about the anxieties, resentments and fears which surge within us.

Psychologists have reminded us for some time that it is important to get into the open the many drives, urges and emotions which strongly influence our thinking and conduct. They grow unhealthy if allowed no expression. To "talk them out" is a catharsis, derived from the Greek *katharsis*, meaning purging or cleansing. Originally, the word had to do with the purification of the emotions through art, but in modern medical terminology it is used to indicate purgation in a much broader sense.

It is advisable to seek an understanding friend or counselor with whom we can "talk out" our resentments without restraint. Expressing the emotion to another person often serves to dissipate its power. We "blow off steam"—a strikingly apt phrase. If the tea kettle simmering cozily above the flame had no outlet, in a matter of time the confined steam would build to a powerful explosion. Similarly, it is dangerous to let the flame of our anger keep our resentments boiling inside. For emotional safety, "talking it out" is a prudent escape.

To put our muscles to work also helps to discharge the emotion of resentment, so to *work it off* is an effective aid. Have we seen anyone so angry that he kicked the chair over which he had stumbled? It was a silly action; even the perpetrator knew it was foolish, especially if he hurt his foot and was forced to limp away. Nevertheless, he was in pursuit of a sound psychological principle, that of relieving emotion through action.

A mother reprimands her child. Rather than sulk at home, he takes out his resentment by kicking a can as he walks moodily down the block. Then he joins in a baseball game on the corner lot. He comes home for the evening meal completely fagged. His resentment has disappeared.

As adults, we cannot kick cans along the street or join in a sandlot game, but there are legitimate physical outlets for our emotion. We can tackle the job of cleaning house with vigor, rearranging the furniture and making the dirt fly. At the end of the day we are exhausted physically, but the house is more attractive and our resentments trouble us less, or not at all. When someone treats us boorishly, instead of vowing vengeance and allowing our animosity to smolder within, we can busy ourselves with the attic or the unsightly garage. After having been courteous to exasperating people for eight hours in the office or store, we can walk hard on our way home, or go to the gymnasium to play handball, pound a punching bag, or plunge into the swimming pool. The more tired our muscles become, the weaker will grow most of our resentments.

A man sixty years of age went to a doctor for a physical checkup. The physician examined him thoroughly and then complimented him on his fine physical condition. "What do you do to stay in such splendid trim?" he inquired.

"Years ago, doctor," the man explained, "my wife and I agreed that if either of us ever became angry, the other would keep out of the way until the mood passed. I determined that in such an instance I would take a walk. Doctor, the outdoor life has kept me in the pink of condition!"

Under certain circumstances, the "outdoor life" may prove an excellent idea! A hike in the woods or a round of golf may do wonders to improve our disposition. Our resentments find it difficult to gnaw as vigorously while we mow the lawn or spade the garden. Working with flowers or growing things has a way of lessening hostilities and assuaging heartaches. What we take out of a garden usually is not as important as the things we leave in it.

A third suggestion in the mastery of resentment is *the use of understanding and imagination.* This includes the ability to put oneself in the other person's place and to understand why he acts as he does. Jane Addams, herself subject to much misunderstanding, once remarked that the most cultivated person was the one who was able to put himself in the place of the greatest number of people. When one acquires the ability to see through another's eyes, resentments do not burn with as hot a flame. When one understands some of the reasons why another acts as he does—the strain he is under, the convictions which motivate him, the burdens he carries,

the anxieties he faces—some of the irritation one feels because of what he says and does begins to slacken. "Let us
be kind to one another," wrote Ian Maclaren, "for most of
us are fighting a hard battle."

The principle works somewhat on the order of the old-
fashioned balance scales. A weight is placed in a pan on one
side of the balance, then the material to be weighed is added
to the pan on the other side until the balance is equal. When
resentment weights the scales, understanding and imagination can help to level the balance.

For instance, when his superior reprimanded the young
man who came to my office, furious resentment filled one
pan in his emotional scale and tilted the balance bar at a
sharp angle. During the course of our conversation, the
young man tried to imagine himself in his superior's place
and to view the situation through his eyes. Although he had
not made the mistake which won the ire of the superintendent, he was objective enough to understand why the superintendent could have thought that it was his error. Moreover,
the mistake had cost the company money. This added a grain
or two of understanding to the superior's side of the scale
and the bar settled slightly toward level.

The young man made the observation that perhaps this
was one in a series of exasperating incidents which his boss
had faced that week and especially that morning. This error
proved to be the straw that broke the camel's back. Thus
the young fellow added another grain or two of understanding to the balance pan.

Perhaps, I reminded him, the supervisor was under fire
from his superiors; that things in his division had not been
going smoothly and, being worried, his nerves were on edge.
Perhaps his wife was ill, or he was concerned about his own
health, or about his son in service. Giving his supervisor the
benefit of the doubt and assuming that he was under pres-

sure placed more weight on the pan of understanding. Thus, by the creative use of imagination and insight, the young man was able to balance the emotional scales and to lessen his feelings of resentment.

This is the kind of understanding for which Robert Burns was pleading when he wrote:

> Then gently scan your brother man,
> Still gentler sister woman;
> Tho' they may gang a kennin wrang,
> To step aside is human:
> One point must still be greatly dark,
> The moving *why* they do it;
> And just as lamely can ye mark
> How far perhaps they rue it.
> Who made the heart, 'tis He alone
> Decidedly can try us:
> He knows each chord, its various tone,
> Each spring, its various bias;
> Then at the balance let's be mute,
> We never can adjust it;
> What's done we partly may compute;
> But know not what's resisted.

In addition to understanding the other person, it lessens resentment to *take an objective look at ourselves.* Is there something in us which irritates others? Do we wield a sharp tongue? Are we quick to assert ourselves, even at the cost of hurting the feelings of others? Do we insist on having things our way? Are we sensitive to criticism? Do we have mannerisms offensive to those about us? An effort to look at ourselves objectively may not give us a completely accurate picture, but it can serve to uncover personality traits which cause others to react to us unfavorably. Having become aware of them, we can proceed to modify or eliminate them.

In a Scottish village lived a half-witted man whose coat

was covered with curious patches—most of them large and glaring. When asked why he wore the patches on his coat, he would reply, "They represent the sins of my neighbors. I'm reminding them of their errors." In the back of the coat squarely between his shoulders was one tiny patch. When questioned about it he would answer, "Oh, that is my own sin. I canna' see it."

When we cease placing the distasteful patches of our personal faults where we cannot see them and bring them around where we can look at them intelligently, we are traveling a road that leads away from resentment.

One patch may be our relation to those about us. Common sense (which is all too uncommon) tells us that we cannot expect everyone to like us, to understand our motives, to make allowances for our foibles, to forgive our quick temper, or to appreciate what we are trying to accomplish. Common sense says that not everyone will be kind, courteous and considerate, and that we must accept people as they are without starting an uninvited crusade to make them over. It warns us to expect a certain amount of dislike and criticism. When Dr. Edward Everett was a famous figure in Boston a few generations ago, an indignant citizen rushed in to see him one evening in a highly agitated condition. A local newspaper had criticized the man and he wanted to know what to do about it. Should he demand a public apology, he wanted to know, or should he sue for damages? Dr. Everett listened quietly and then counseled, "What should you do? Why, my dear sir, do nothing! Half the people who read the paper did not see the article about you. Half of those who read it did not understand it. Half of those who understood it did not believe it. Half of those who believed it are of no consequence, anyway. You should do nothing!" [1]

The application of common sense dismisses similarly many

of the things that irritate us. We can refuse to let them rile us. They are not worth the trouble.

Moreover, those who have been most successful in curbing animosity *have used resentment as a teacher*. They ask in each trying situation, "What can this irritation teach me about myself? What is the reason for this resentment? Something constructive can come from this; what can I learn to make me a more mature person?" In adopting this attitude, they are able to shape their antagonisms into allies which work for them, rather than enemies which war against them.

The poet Robert Browning learned early in life to use his resentments as teachers. As a youth he had fallen in love with a Miss Eliza Flower. She was older than he and on her part the emotion seems to have been a maternal affection and a desire to help this talented young man. His love for her, however, inspired him to write the first of his published works, a poem called *Pauline*. With an author's pride, he sent a copy to a friendly critic who praised it and passed it on to a rising young critic, John Stuart Mill. Mill did not react kindly to the poem. "With considerable poetic powers," he said, "the writer seems to me possessed with a more intense and morbid self-consciousness than I ever knew in any human being."

At first, Robert Browning was shocked and crushed. Had he been a lesser person, he could have burned with resentment against John Stuart Mill. But he did a wiser thing; he decided to take the criticism constructively. He *was* self-conscious, he admitted to himself. If he did not correct this defect, it would mar all he wrote. How well he succeeded in combatting this tendency his later poetry attests.[2]

When there is reason for resentment, it is senseless to allow ourselves to flare with anger or to grow sullen with ill will. Like Browning we can look at the situation objectively to learn if it can point out weaknesses which we can correct.

Another method which has proved successful is to banish resentment *by an act of will,* deliberately to shut the door of the mind against the things which irritate and to refuse to let them in. Each of us has this power, if we exercise it. It performs the function of a fire curtain in a theater. If a fire breaks out on the stage or in the dressing rooms, the curtain is dropped to prevent the flames from reaching the audience. Similarly, it is possible to drop the curtain of one's will and prohibit the fire of resentment from reaching the auditorium of one's life. Whenever irritations rise to torment us, we drop the curtain; we dismiss them summarily and refuse them entrance into our thoughts. If time after time we persist in this attitude, steadfastly denying them to pass the protective curtain of our will, eventually they will cease to torment us.

The more successful we are at banishing resentment by strength of will, the better balanced individuals we are, and the more likable. Dr. Donald A. Laird tested this fact in a class at Colgate University. He asked the students to write down as rapidly as they could the initials of the persons whom they disliked. After thirty seconds, some listed as many as fourteen sets of initials, while others could think only of one. Dr. Laird uncovered this interesting commentary—the men who wrote the longest lists were themselves among the most unpopular on the campus! Evidently resentment and ill will do something distasteful to the personalities of those who hold them.

Melvin J. Evans, human relations expert and director of *Democracy in Action,* believes this to be so; in fact, he refers to resentment as a disease. He wrote [3] of an interview with a man named John who was so filled with resentment that he balked at being interviewed. After some persuasion, he came in and sat down glumly, glaring as if the conference were an insult. His response to attempts at conversation was an occasional grunt. Suddenly he blurted, "I know I've got a rotten rating, but what business is it of yours? Everybody hates me and I hate everybody, but I do my work! I do what I'm paid for! I hate this company and I'm going to quit, but it's none of your business!"

Perhaps he expected the counselor to sympathize with him and beg him to stay, but instead Mr. Evans said simply, "Why don't you quit? If I felt as you do, I'd certainly quit!"

This took the man by surprise and set him back on his heels for a moment. He was desperately unhappy, had put himself in an unbearable position and did not know which way to turn. The executive followed his momentary advantage. "Let's assume you're going to quit. But if I were you I'd certainly get rid of your state of mind before I left. If you carry all this poison to another job you'll ruin it, too." Then the flood gates broke and for an hour the embittered workman talked in a steady torrent. "It was just like draining an abscess," Mr. Evans remarked.

A year or so earlier John and three others had "blown their tops" at the superintendent and had demanded his discharge. This angered the president of the firm and he let all four of them go. Then, realizing that he had acted hastily, he rehired John. But he had not taken time to heal the emotional rift.

"Often we fail to see the stark reality of these ulcers of the soul and expect them to disappear," Mr. Evans commented. "They are much more apt to grow and develop in virulence. What is the antidote? . . . If we see to it that our minds are filled with positive, constructive thoughts, there is no room for negative, antagonistic thinking. Our difficulty lies in the fact that we have not learned to prepare, on a day-to-day basis, for these emotional storms. When they hit us, we are helpless and pay a very heavy penalty. . . . We simply must not permit our lives to be pushed around and controlled by outward circumstances. The thoughts which habitually occupy our minds are like the white corpuscles in the blood. They prevent infection and keep the whole personality sane and healthy."

Resentment acts like a poison in the bloodstream. It had infected John, had reduced his efficiency, and had affected every area of his life. The company management had been faulty in handling a delicate situation, but the man himself was the big loser. Although he still was doing his work, his effectiveness was impaired, he had become an outcast in the organization, and a skilled operator was on the way out.

After·the explosion of pent-up emotion, the counselor suggested a daily program of meditation and study, including prayer and the use of the Scriptures. The man accepted the suggestions readily and initiated a systematic plan to replace bitterness with good will and understanding. His wife and family were only too happy to co-operate. Within two weeks the change in his personality was remarkable.

He had a crippled friend who had become despondent. With the exuberance of a blind man who had learned to see, he passed along his daily plan to his friend and took huge delight in watching him develop. "In all relationships," Mr. Evans concluded, "John became a constructive person—a positive therapeutic for discord and antagonism."

It is not something unique that human personality can change and expand when it lays aside resentment, especially with the constructive aid of good will, prayer and a dynamic use of the Scriptures. Almost nineteen hundred years ago, St. Paul explained this same technique to the people in the little church at Ephesus. "Let all bitterness, and wrath, and anger, and clamour, and evil speaking, be put away from you," he advised them, "with all malice: and be ye kind one to another. . . ." Bitterness, wrath, anger, clamor, slander, malice—what an evil brood! If we carry them locked in our hearts, it is small wonder that they poison the spirit, leaving us unhappy, tense and ill. If we long for well-being and happiness, it is essential to clean them out and to drop the curtain against them so that they cannot return to plague us.

Likewise, we free ourselves from resentment *by an act of faith*. Knowingly or unknowingly, we select the personal attitudes by which we live. Religious conviction can give power to the will, as the experience of the unfortunate workman illustrates. When we live "as if" kindness, tolerance, forgiveness and trust are more important than vindictiveness and hatred—then they are.

"If selfish people try to take advantage of you, cross them off your list, but don't try to get even. When you try to get even, you hurt yourself more than you hurt the other fellow." These are not the words of a sentimentalist; they appeared in a bulletin issued by the Milwaukee Police Department. Grudge-bearing and maliciousness are forms of suffering which harm the one who bears them more than those against whom they are directed. The only persons with whom we should try to get even are those who have helped us.

This act of faith includes at least three elements. First, it is *an attitude of undiscourageable good will* assumed deliberately because we are convinced that it is more practical than resentment. Second, it calls for *acts of kindness* toward the one against whom we could direct hostility. Such kindly acts give substance to the attitude of good will. Third, it is essential *to pray* for those "who despitefully use you." Such prayer aids us as well as the object of our petitions. The one who harms us needs our compassion. His vindictive attitude cankers his spirit; the acids of animosity curdle his better nature; hostility steals his joy. Prayer releases spiritual forces which help liberate him from such bondage, and at the same time it saves us from the same destructive emotions. Sincere and earnest prayer for another makes it impossible to hold resentment for long, as we can discover for ourselves.

The apostle Peter once came to the Master with a question. "How many times shall I forgive my brother," he asked, "seven times?" To the ancient Jewish mind, seven was the perfect number. "No, not seven times," Jesus replied, "but seventy times seven." Peter was to place no limits on his spirit of forgiveness. Jesus knew the havoc that animosity can work in a man's inner life. He was aware of what a seething cauldron of hates could do to poison efficiency, happiness and peace. He understood how a burden of vindictiveness could weigh down the spirit, until the person who bore it became a problem to others and a puzzle to himself. He knew that only the immature personality takes a chronically hostile attitude toward the world, wears a constant chip on his shoulder, has an elephant's memory for past slights and finds secret enjoyment in another's discomforts and defeats. By an act of faith and an attitude of unswerving good will he would remove all such evils.

How it works in practical experience is revealed in a radio drama, based on a real life experience, which told the tale of a boy who hated his brutal, drunken, anger-torn father. The boy's life was filled with a strange sense of dissatisfaction and unhappiness. He had the sensation that he had slipped his moorings and was drifting.

As the drama unfolded, the boy underwent a moving religious experience. Afterward, he knelt and prayed that he might have power to forgive his father. His prayer was answered; the bitterness which had soured the joy in his life disappeared, and he came to understand that "hate is twisted love." His resentment turned to compassion for the bedeviled man whose anger tore at him like a wild beast and drove

him to despicable things. The boy's newly won insight conquered his sense of aimlessness and gave him compassion to
aid his pitiable father.

Like this boy, we are wise to open the door of forgiveness.
Life is too sweet and too short to spend it nursing wrongs or
bearing grudges. Once we have placed our enemy's faults on
the altar, figuratively speaking, together with our forgiveness, it is essential *to walk away and leave them there.* Then,
if our experience resembles that of many others, a strange
lightness of spirit envelops us, as if a burden has been lifted.
Another's dislike or antagonism fails to disturb us deeply,
for compassion grants an understanding that leads to pity
rather than to revenge.

A final constructive method in overcoming resentment is
to identify ourselves with an important cause. When we are
doing something which we consider supremely worth while,
slights and animosities do not perturb us unduly. Since our
interest is centered elsewhere, we can ignore them.

When the Wright brothers began to experiment seriously
with the airplane, they met with a torrent of criticism and
abuse. Some people accused them of being insane. "It is
absurd to think that a machine heavier than air can fly,"
their critics declared. "If God had intended for man to fly,
he would have placed wings on his shoulders. Moreover, if
anyone ever does fly, it will not be in Dayton, Ohio!"

The Wright brothers paid no attention to the critics. They
did not grow resentful, fight back or quit. What they were
doing was too important to be concerned with what people
thought or said; they worked harder than ever on their experiments. Finally the day came when they launched the
little Kitty Hawk into the air, and the age of aviation had
begun.

If we wish to wear an armor against resentments, it is
important to plunge into a useful work. When we commit

ourselves completely to an essential service, there is little
time and less inclination to worry about what people say in
ridicule or criticism.

> They say.
> What do they say?
> Let them say.

The opinion of our critics is not important. We are too busy
to listen.

Certainly there is no lack of great causes to claim us. We
live in "an age on ages telling." Gigantic forces for good and
evil are locked in a death struggle to determine the course
of future generations. If absorption in noble undertakings
can free us from resentment, there is enough urgent need in
the world to kill resentment altogether! Yet, when we look
about, it is astounding to note how many people seem con-
tent to dodder on their flat-footed ways insensible to the
gallantry which could command them, to the commitments
which could give rich meaning to their lives. No bugles blow
for them; they have no date with destiny. No thrilling cause
rallies their powers or calls forth their deepest potentials.

In the meantime, people glare and snarl at one another
like animals. Heart failures increase, animosities and fears
poison our attitudes, and mental hospitals are filled to overflowing. We are fast becoming a nation of neurotics. Sur-
feited with pleasures, we miss happiness and fall prey to
boredom and resentment.

Wendell Phillips' stinging denunciations of slavery made
him a leader of the abolitionist forces. When he was an old
man, a young enthusiast exclaimed, "Mr. Phillips, I wish I
had lived in your time so that I could have joined your
crusade!" The old man's shoulders straightened. Pointing
through a window toward a sordid section of the city, he
said, "Young man, you are living in God's time and your

time. If what you see as you look out of that window does not arouse you, you would not have been aroused in my time or in any other time."

He might well be speaking the word to us. As we look at our world, if what we see does not arouse us from our lethargies with a concern great enough to consume our touchiness, then no age on earth could have been able to do so. Once we throw ourselves into the arena and champion a responsibility noble enough to absorb our fullest energies, we sign the death warrant to most of our resentments.

CHAPTER X

Overcoming Our Anxieties

In the Sermon on the Mount, when Jesus said, "Do not be anxious about your life," his comment was more pertinent to our day than in the age he phrased it. In league with fear and anxiety, modern tensions sabotage our peace and steal our serenity.

Tenseness and uncertainty mark our age. Western civilization has been characterized as a shattered atom, a deflated dollar and a worried look. A large industrial concern discovered that nine out of ten cases of workers' inefficiency were caused by worry. An analysis of the records of a well-known medical clinic revealed that 35 per cent of all illnesses treated in the clinic started with anxiety. A life insurance company reported that four out of five nervous breakdowns began not in actual events but with worry. Heart failure and diseases resulting from hypertension rapidly are becoming the major killers among all ailments. Dr. Charles Mayo of the famous Mayo Clinic in Rochester, Minnesota, says, "Worry affects the circulation, the heart, the glands, the whole nervous system and profoundly affects the health. I have never known a man who died from overwork, but many who have died from doubt."

These facts are even more startling when we realize that a baby is born with only two normal fears, the fear of loud noises and the dread of falling. All other anxieties are acquired. These run the gamut from a feeling of uneasiness

166

about walking under a ladder or of Friday the thirteenth to an exaggerated fear of death. None of them "just happen." We learn them in the same manner that we learn every habit, good or bad. We nurture them, practice them and allow them to develop—sometimes to frightening proportions.

Habits of worry and fear can gain such a pernicious hold on our thinking and attitudes that we extricate ourselves only after resolute effort. A boy watched a plumber removing a pipe. The plumber's face contorted with the effort and perspiration dripped from his forearms as he strained at the stubborn joint. The boy observed, "It's hard work being a plumber, isn't it?" The plumber stopped his work, looked down at the lad and mopped the sweat from his face. "If it were easy, son, everyone would be a plumber."

If it were easy to be free from anxiety, no one would worry. Even those who are most addicted realize that the habit of overanxiety is harmful. It is not by choice that we acquire a worried attitude. We have no desire to drag as slaves linked to the chariot wheels of worry. We say, "I shall refuse to give way to my fears and anxieties. I shall cease to worry about tomorrow. I am determined to be a serene and poised person." Thus we try to break the chains of dread; thus we attempt to pull ourselves out of the quagmire of apprehension by our own bootstraps. We struggle until our nerves quiver under the strain, but it does little good. Soon we slip back into the worry pattern and are as consumed with anxiety as before.

The fault lies, not in that we have selected an impossible goal, but in choosing the wrong method to achieve it. It is useless to attempt to reach Florida from New York by traveling east, no matter how far we may journey; Florida does not lie in that direction. Nor can we gain serenity of spirit by screwing up our determination or by flaying our wills. Freedom from anxiety does not lie in that direction. Yet it is possible to overcome an affinity for worry by the application of certain common-sense attitudes and principles.

The first suggestion is to *face our anxieties realistically.* We shall discover that most of the things about which we worry never occur. Hans Christian Andersen, who wrote wonderful fairy tales for children, never seemed able to free himself from anxiety. He had a horror of illness; his imagination would magnify the slightest scratch or pimple into a fatal malady. A doctor who knew the storyteller intimately found Andersen trembling with anxiety one day because a friend was half an hour late. What agonies the unhappy author endured in that period of waiting no one can surmise. He was certain that his friend had met a violent end, or was injured in a traffic accident, or smashed in a collision, or torn to bits by an explosion. In his mind, Andersen pictured his friend dying in terrible suffering; he saw the corpse, crushed and bleeding, carried home on a stretcher.

"He would have escaped from the horrifying sight but could not," wrote the doctor. "His feet seemed rooted to the spot. He was obliged to stay and see the body of his dead friend put in a decent coffin, and consigned to its last resting place. Then he pictured himself sitting down with streaming eyes, writing letters of condolences to the sorrowing relatives —and at that very moment, who should come up with smiling face and outstretched arms but the very friend whose death he had so vividly realized and who, on perceiving poor Andersen's terrible state of agitation, was not only abject in his apologies, but registered a mental oath never to keep him waiting again." [1]

Before condemning Hans Christian Andersen for his vivid but senseless anxieties, let us ask ourselves if we are guilty of the same needless agitation. Do we allow our imaginations to run away from us and to picture dreadful results? Do we envision the worst and then convince ourselves that it is bound to occur? If so, common sense will tell us that we are borrowing useless trouble.

An author with a tendency to worry, but blessed with a sense of humor, analyzed his anxieties into a "Worry Table" [2] and divided his concerns into five classifications. First, there were the worries about disasters which, as later events proved, never happened. These accounted for 40 per cent of his anxieties. Second, worries about decisions he had made in the past and about which now he could do nothing included 30 per cent. Third, worries about possible sickness and a dreaded nervous breakdown, which did not materialize, covered 12 per cent of his anxieties. Fourth, worries about his children and friends arising from the fact that he forgot that "they had an ordinary amount of common sense," provided another 10 per cent. Finally, there were the anxieties which had real foundation. These composed only 8 per cent of the total! Ninety-two per cent of his anxieties were needless.

In general, these figures apply to our personal situation. About nine tenths of our anxieties are groundless. If we find this statement difficult to accept, we can make the experiment of keeping track of the principal things about which we worry. Jot down each anxiety in a diary or on a slip of paper and place it in a convenient file. At the end of two weeks, eliminate the worries which in that length of time have proved baseless. Retain the others and keep adding new anxieties to the list. At the end of the month, remove the worries about which you no longer are concerned. Prolong this experiment over the course of a year, if need be, but a shorter time should prove that roughly nine tenths of the things about which we worry fail to happen. Also, we shall discover that these needless worries cause us as much trouble as if they were based on fact! It should be encouraging to realize that the misfortunes we most dread rarely happen.

But what of the percentage of anxieties that prove to be well founded—are they not sufficient to cause grave concern? They are, to be sure, but fortunately when the things we dread actually happen, usually they are not as difficult to handle as we anticipate. A woman shook her husband awake in the middle of the night and whispered that she heard a burglar downstairs. Sleepily her husband descended the stairs to find himself looking into the muzzle of a gun. "Hands up!" commanded the robber. "Keep still and hand over your valuables, and nothing will happen to you."

The man assured the burglar that there would be no outcry and that he was welcome to the silver. "However," he continued, "I wish that you would do one favor before you go. I want you to come upstairs to meet my wife. She has been looking for you every night for twenty years!"

Suppose that we are worried about an operation that we dread and have postponed as long as possible. Now we must go through with it and the prospect frightens us. It is not pleasant to anticipate, but, if we are like thousands of others, we shall discover inner resources to meet the emergency. Afterward, the experience will not seem nearly as dreadful as our worries pictured it to be. At least, it will give a convenient subject for conversation!

Look back to the time when we transferred to another school, or assumed the responsibilities of a strange, new job. We still recall how fearful we were and how we dreaded the change. From the vantage of the intervening years, we smile at the anxiety we felt then. We were able to make the adjustment; in fact we gained happiness and self-confidence through the experience. Facing our anxieties realistically, we eliminate many of them and find courage to meet the rest without quavering.

A second suggestion is to *maintain a constructive view-point toward the things that trouble us.* There are at least two attitudes to take toward any situation: one is negative and defeatist; the other is positive and hopeful. One person, looking at a glass partially filled with water, remarks that the glass is half empty; another declares that the glass is half full. The object in each instance is the same; the attitude is different. The sanguine viewpoint shuts out needless anxiety. When a mighty river rises to flood level, it cannot inundate the cities along its course unless it overflows the levees or breaks through a weakness in the dikes. Although we may face a flood of anxieties, they cannot submerge our spirits as long as we maintain a stout high wall to keep them out. A realistic, constructive approach helps immeasurably to keep the wall tall and watertight, thus preventing our cares from swamping us. We can approach each day with an attitude of confidence, certain that at least a few rays of sunshine will reach us even in the gloomiest hour, and that the most diffi-cult situation has a solution.

Samuel F. B. Morse, the inventor of the telegraph, labored for years on his invention and invested all his financial re-sources in its development. A bill was introduced in Congress to authorize the expenditure of federal funds to continue the experiments. If the bill failed to pass, it would be impossible for him to keep working and the efforts of a lifetime would end in failure. Morse sat in the Senate gallery throughout the day and long into the evening. Finally, two senators came to him with the news that the situation looked hope-less. Time was almost gone and a great many bills remained for consideration.

The inventor left the gallery and returned to the hotel, planning to leave Washington the following day. Then, in a sentence that reveals the spirit in which he had trained him-self to deal with anxiety and failure, he wrote in a letter to a friend, "Knowing from long experience from whence my help comes in hours of difficulty, I soon disposed of all my cares and slept as quietly as a child."

The next morning, Morse learned that his bill had been lumped with a number of others and had passed just before the deadline at midnight! The future lay open before him.

Jesus, the master of successful living, emphasized this spirit of positive trust. "Consider the birds of the heavens and the flowers of the field," he said to those about him. "It is evident, is it not, that God protects them. You are of much more value than they; be sure that your heavenly Father will care for you. Therefore, don't be anxious, saying, 'What shall we eat, or drink, or wear?' Your heavenly Father knows that you have need of all these things. Seek ye first his kingdom and his righteousness and all these things shall be yours as well."

People often interpret this portion in St. Matthew's gospel to mean that mundane, everyday things like food, drink and clothing are unimportant and that the spiritual-minded individual should ignore them to concentrate on other-worldly concerns. This is the opposite of what Jesus meant. He was pointing out that we need not be concerned unduly about life's necessities, giving them more attention than they deserve, not because they are unimportant, *but because they are essential.* "Your heavenly Father knows that you need them all."

Jesus is saying, "God provides the essentials of life; trust Him to make provision for these necessities. Think trustfully. Don't absorb yourself in items of such vital importance that human existence cannot be sustained without them. God is sufficient for things and you can trust Him utterly. Therefore, face each day with courage and assurance."

Instead of receiving the release from anxiety which such an attitude of assurance brings, many of us have the unfortunate habit of looking at the dark side of things, as did the farmer with his chickens. An acquaintance complimented him on the fine brood of chickens scratching in the barnyard. The farmer drew a long face. "It ain't as good as you think," he said. "The old hen hatched out twelve chicks and all but eleven up and died on me!"

Our lives are shaped not so much by what happens to us as by the attitude we take toward that which happens. If we raise lightning rods of anxiety, we are bound to attract thunderbolts of difficulty. If we brood about disaster, it is likely to seek us out. We build molehills of inconvenience into mountains of disaster. Heartbreaks, disappointments and unfavorable circumstances do affect life, of course, but it lies within our power to channel the effect.

In his letter to the Philippians, St. Paul writes, "In nothing be anxious; but in everything by prayer and supplication with thanksgiving let your bequests be made known unto God." *In nothing* be anxious—*in everything* be thankful; according to the Apostle, the method to eliminate each anxiety is to put a thanksgiving in its place.

Consider how the principle works. In each difficulty is something for which to be grateful, if we seek it out. What keeps us tense and anxious? Are we worried about a son or daughter? We thank God, in the first place, that we have a child about whom to worry! Many lonely hearts have been denied this privilege, or have had young lives snatched from them by death. We give thanks, also, that there is a strong and patient Hand which guides young people when their ways wind through dark valleys or in slippery places. Are we anxious about the future? Look back at the course our lives have followed. Are there not points where, beyond our own skill or wisdom, we made the right decision or avoided a pit of serious difficulty into which we easily could have fallen? Are there not periods in which, like Robert Louis

Stevenson in a crucial incident in his life, we came about like a well-handled ship? We recognized that the hand on the helm was not our own, but that of an unknown Steersman. In honesty, no one can deny the reality of such incidents in his personal experience, nor explain them away as coincidence. This being true, it is possible to cover anxiety about the future with a thanksgiving. We offer gratitude and take courage; what has happened in the past can and will happen again if our personal attitudes are such that they allow it to happen.

We can review our entire list of anxieties in this fashion. As we wrap each in a thanksgiving we may notice that our worries tend to grow smaller—or to vanish altogether.

A third suggestion toward the conquest of anxiety is *to live in the present,* refusing to borrow trouble from the future. One day I watched a bricklayer and his helper building a wall. It was the helper's responsibility to supply the bricks from a great pile which lay near the base of the wall. The thought occurred that most of us could learn a lesson from the way he tackled his job. What if the helper had said to himself, "I must lift that huge pile of bricks to the top of the wall, carrying them up that ladder. The harder I work the higher the wall grows and the farther I must climb. I don't see how I can accomplish it. There must be at least two tons of bricks in that pile. I am not up to lifting such a tremendous weight. The job is too much for me!"

Many times we approach our jobs in this manner. We see them *in toto* and they look mountainous. We tell ourselves, "Those problems are much too big for me to handle. It's more responsibility than I can manage. Look at all I must do today! There's no use for me to attempt it; I know I'll fail." Thus we are defeated before we start.

But the bricklayer's helper was more sensible. He did not attempt to carry the whole pile of bricks at once. He placed only as many bricks in his V-shaped hod as he could carry, hoisted them to his shoulder, walked up the ladder and placed them at the bricklayer's side. Then he returned for another load. In this manner the pile of bricks slowly diminished, the bricklayer was constantly supplied and the wall continued to rise. Instead of worrying about carrying our entire responsibility or solving our total stack of problems, is it not more sensible to approach them as the bricklayer's helper dealt with the pile of bricks?

Moreover, if we live in the present, concentrating on the cares and burdens of today, we shall be better fitted to take care of what may come tomorrow and the day after that. Our main concern is with today. Tomorrow is a sealed book. We gain inner poise when we do not fret about it or dread its coming. *Today* is ours, ours to use to the fullest, meeting each individual duty as it comes. Then we do not add tomorrow's cares to our current burdens. Anxiety about the future does not lighten tomorrow's load, but it lessens our adequacy for today.

Another method is to drive out anxiety through *constructive action*. As with resentment, to "work it out" discharges excessive energy successfully. One reason why there was less mental illness three generations ago is because it was the age of personal handicraft. Many fears and worries are the result of too much subjective analysis and not enough physical activity. Purposeful action serves as an outlet for pent-up emotions. The battle-tested soldier finds it harder to hate the enemy than the person at home who lacks the soldier's opportunity to discharge the emotion through action. The individual with many worries, who feels incompetent and unsure of himself, usually is one who has not converted enough of his energies into physical expression.

Before the World Series in 1928, Carl Sandburg interviewed Babe Ruth for the *Chicago Daily News*. "People

come and ask you what's your system for hitting home runs
—is that so?" Sandburg asked him.

"Yes," the immortal Babe replied, "and all I can tell 'em
is, I pick a good one and sock it. I get back to the dugout
and they ask me what it was I hit and I tell 'em I don't
know except it looked good."

Had he stopped to analyze each pitch, or questioned his
ability to hit it, the ball would have been in the catcher's
mitt while the bat was still on his shoulder. When the pitch
came in right, he *acted* with devastating results to the oppos-
ing team.

Ty Cobb, another of baseball's immortals, set more records
in his twenty-four years in the majors than any competitor
who ever lived. A group of sports writers interviewed him
near the end of one season. "We've watched you all season,"
they told him, "and we've discovered that you have eleven
different ways of sliding into second base. At what point between first and second do you decide which of those eleven
ways you'll use?"

Ty flashed back, "I never think about it. I just slide."

As with these stars, the difference for us between success
and failure, dissatisfaction and happiness, contentment and
uncertainty, often depends on constructive action. In seeking
peace of mind, it is wise to pour our lives into something
which requires physical effort and which serves someone else,
or a good cause. It burns up the energy which we are
tempted to pour into worry. No matter how big or insurmountable our problems may seem, we start ridding ourselves of confusion when we take one little step toward the
solution. We try something. Having acted and made a start,
we can try again—and keep on trying. Even our mistakes
bring us closer to our goal.

Once a philosophy professor found his son in the bathroom
with the floor flooded. He stood thinking, trying to picture

how the accident had happened. After a few seconds the boy cried, "Dad, this is no time to philosophize. It's time to mop!"

There is a time to think and to plan, of course, but likewise there is a time to act. The weakness in many emotionally upset persons is that they spend too much time in worry about their problems and not enough energy in wielding the mop. If there is one central secret of overcoming anxiety, it is to form the habit of doing those things that distracted people do not like to do.

A final secret is *to use our faith constructively,* remembering that faith is not something we acquire, but something we have. In the last analysis, freedom from anxiety is but faith in action. When we live "as if" there were no cause for worry, assume a confident attitude toward our difficulties and tackle them realistically, it lies within our power to conquer our concerns.

A portion of a letter from a banker reveals how a positive faith changed his future from defeat to triumph. "During the depression," he wrote, "after the first World War when the bottom dropped out of everything, I had over three million dollars of real estate mortgages in the hands of investors, loans that I had made in Kansas and had placed with eastern and local investors. It looked as if I were not going to be able to keep faith with my clients. I began to read the Bible and pray as I never prayed before. This passage brought me the peace and confidence that carried me through without loss of any consequence to anyone: 'Thou wilt keep him in perfect peace whose mind is stayed on thee; because he trusteth in thee.' "

He buried that verse of Scripture deep in his subconscious. Its assurance brought him courage and hope. Thus fortified, his faith provided the confidence and steadiness he needed to see him through his difficulties. "After I felt this peace and confidence, I had faith that if I did my part, everything would work out satisfactorily. In other words, I prayed as if everything depended on God and worked as if everything depended on me. It would be impossible for me to operate my business without faith," he concluded. "Religion is a wonderful thing, for it gives one courage and strength to go forward, knowing that all things work together for good to those who love and serve God as they should."

When, like this banker, we test our faith in the crucible of experience and discover that it provides rich resources in mastering our problems, such assurance loosens the grip of our anxieties. We become convinced that we do not fight our battles alone, that power other than our own is available for those who have the courage and humility to claim it, and that a kindly Providence watches over our ways beyond our comprehension.

Oliver Cromwell once sent a secretary to the Continent on an important secret mission. The night before sailing, the secretary tossed in his bed, unable to sleep. According to custom, a servant slept in the same room and, awakened by his master's restlessness, he inquired why he could not sleep. The secretary replied, "I am terribly afraid that something will go wrong with the responsibility which has been given into my keeping."

Hesitatingly, the servant inquired, "Master, may I ask a question?"

"Of course you may," the secretary assured him.

"Master, did God rule the world before we were born?"

"Most assuredly He did."

"And will He rule it again after we are dead?"

"Certainly God will rule His world after we are dead," the great man answered, puzzled by the conversation.

His servant paused for a moment. "Then, master, why can we not let Him rule the present also?"

Cromwell's secretary saw the point and faith revived within him. Soon he was sound asleep. The principle is as true in our day as in the time of Cromwell. When we exercise our faith constructively, trusting in the Almighty to share our cares, anxieties diminish and lose their power.

CHAPTER XI

When Trouble Troubles Us

IMAGINE yourself sixty-two years old, without funds, dying of cancer and haunted by the knowledge that you are leaving your family without financial security. Such was the fate of Ulysses S. Grant, one-time victorious general and twice President of the United States.

Grant had been a man of moderate financial circumstances, but after his retirement from public life he lived beyond his income. Then, in an attempt to recoup his fortunes, he fell into the hands of a certain Ferdinand Ward, called the "young Napoleon of Wall Street." But Ward turned out to be a swindler and Grant lost what money he had. Shortly thereafter, he learned that he had cancer of the throat and had but a few months to live. Had he given up in utter defeat, leaving the members of his family to fend for themselves after his death, it would have been understandable. But he still possessed the fortitude which had made him famous on the battlefield. Instead of succumbing to weakness and pain, he started to write his memoirs. Although his affliction worsened, he continued to write doggedly. Eight months later, when the end came, he had completed nearly two volumes. The income from these volumes subsequently netted almost half a million dollars for his family. Here was a man who refused to let misfortune crush him.

This incident from the life of Ulysses S. Grant centers attention on a problem which we all face eventually. Sooner

or later, each of us shoulders his share of trouble, for, as the
Book of Job declares, "Man is born unto trouble, as the
sparks fly upward."

In the achievement of happiness, it is essential to transform troubles into triumphs. One of the first steps is to *gain
a proper perspective on our difficulties*. Such a perspective
grants an objectivity which makes it possible to deal with
them more intelligently. One of the most effective ways to
gain such a perspective is to look away from our own difficulties and to note the hardships which others are called to
endure. From such a vantage point usually we discover that
our personal troubles are not as large as we had assumed.
Any rabbi, priest or pastor will admit that, when tempted to
feel sorry for himself, all he need do is to visit certain homes
in his parish. He returns to his study convinced that his yoke
is easy and his burdens are light when compared to those
which others are bearing with cheer, faith and fortitude.

In the Korean struggle, tales describing the wretched
plight of the civilian population stirred our sympathy. What
if we had been in business in Seoul, with our shop shattered
and our merchandise carried away? What if we had been a
housewife in one of the little villages made rubble in the
path of the war? What if we had been the parent of a bewildered and half-starved child, shivering in the Korean
cold? In the light of the tragedies which agonize our age, do
not our own troubles shrink in comparison?

It is wise not to let our difficulties loom larger than they
should. A man vacationing in the mountains burst out of the
woods in a desperate sprint, hurled himself into the cabin,
slammed the door and leaned panting against it. "What is
the trouble?" asked his startled wife. He managed to gasp
that a fierce bear was trailing him. The wife looked out of
the window and started to laugh. "You were needlessly
frightened, dear," she chided him. "It wasn't a bear following

you, but only a friendly dog." After glancing to see for himself, the man grumbled, "The way he was stomping around in the underbrush I would have sworn that he was a bear!"

Are we guilty of magnifying our trials in similar fashion? When "stomping around in the underbrush," often they sound more terrifying than they really are. When we are able to maintain a sense of balance, not allowing them to grow out of proportion, it prevents them from looming larger than they should. Then we "don't make tragedies of trifles, don't shoot butterflies with rifles."

A second phase in gaining perspective is to ask ourselves, honestly and objectively, how much we have added to our troubles by the attitude we have taken toward them. We confront real difficulty, to be sure, but have we increased the trouble by the spirit in which we have faced it?

A woman was at her wit's end in dealing with her husband. He was a generous man; in fact, that was the crux of the problem. He was so big-hearted that he helped others from his limited income so lavishly that often his own family were left in want. Moreover, he shunned personal responsibility, particularly in matters pertaining to the home. In trying to correct the situation, the wife's attitudes only deepened the trouble. Intermittently she nagged, stormed, threatened, assumed the role of a "persecuted-wife-suffering-in-silence," or gave way to self-pity. Her husband became sullen and then defiant. The couple were on the brink of divorce.

At this point they talked with some older friends whom they respected and who were able to give them sound counsel. They discussed the difficulties thoroughly. The husband's mistakes were pointed out to him sympathetically but firmly. With equal understanding and firmness, the wife was made aware of the ways in which she, by mishandling the situation, had accentuated the difficulties between her husband

and herself. Certain common-sense procedures were outlined for each to follow. Since they loved each other devotedly in spite of their differences, both were willing to attack their problems in a new sense of co-operation. This proved to be the turning point of their marital life. They still face the problems which any normal couple must meet, but they have learned that the spirit in which they meet them makes a substantial difference. They know that when they take a loving, co-operative attitude toward their problems and toward each other, their difficulties begin to diminish.

Although our individual problem may not be a well-meaning but financially foolish husband, to face it in a balanced and understanding attitude will aid in solving it, whatever it may be. Perhaps the problem is that of health. Has our tenseness added to the load which mind and body must carry? A relaxed and cheerful frame of mind often can free the normal processes of the body to combat illness with added efficiency. Our organs and nerves, our sinews and tissues are far stronger and more reliant than we may assume. The normal state of our bodies is not illness but health; every physical organism—our blood, our glands, our body chemicals—unites as a team against illness. Our bodies resemble a fortified city, each corpuscle and cell at its post in defense of the citadel. Any physician can illustrate from his practice the amazing resourcefulness of the body in combating disease or injury.

In one respect, our bodies are like modern skyscrapers. According to a successful architect, when he plans a building he provides not merely for the normal stress which the building must stand, but multiplies his estimate by three, six, or even twelve times. Then he feels that the building will be safe, no matter what may happen. The architect calls this added protection "the margin of safety."

The human body, too, has its "margin of safety." Within

it are capacities and powers capable of bearing stress far beyond that which normally it is called to bear. When troubled with ill health, or when our bodily resources seem low, we show wisdom in not adding to the strain by assuming an attitude of undue anxiety. We can assure ourselves that we have within powerful forces of protection, regeneration and healing. They already are at work to restore complete health. We must teach ourselves to depend on them.

It is possible to become our own worst enemies in this matter. Distraught and tense, we can overlook these hidden resources of renewal and strength. It is possible to block the flow of these health-giving forces by chronic fear, worry or overstimulation. If we harbor anxiety, it seeps through our thinking, colors our attitudes, damages our personalities and causes us unwittingly to house a phantom. When we confront the extent to which fear ravages personality, it seems evident that to eradicate it from modern existence would be to abolish one of the most powerful enemies of mental health and personal happiness. Our task each day is to remind ourselves that our resources are greater than we think and to *know* that we are sufficient for whatever emergencies may arise. A creative faith, which refuses to borrow trouble and enables us to see "the best that glimmers thro' the worst," releases the inner powers essential to carefree and confident living.

Moreover, a sense of perspective assures us that the present state, as bad as it may be, cannot last forever. This assurance aids in giving the pluck and perseverance which steer us successfully past our difficulties. Long ago, according to a legend, an Oriental monarch wore a ring on which were inscribed these words, "This, too, shall pass away." In the midst of trouble, the phrase served to bring him comfort and courage. The words are similar to a sentiment my grandmother used to express. When difficulties beset her and the road ahead seemed rough, she would remark, "Everything is always over." The thought gave her patience and helped her to hold on until the trying situation changed. The phrase may appear foolish, but personally it has fortified me when such help was needed.

No matter how grievous the present or foreboding the future, in time it will pass away. Often the change comes more quickly than we believe possible. Every difficult trial comes to an end, if we hold on with patience and courage, and refuse to give in. Such certainty can strengthen us when beset by trouble.

In addition to gaining perspective, a second resource is to *see our troubles as opportunities.* Instead of viewing them through the spectacles of consternation, simply to see them as a challenge is to take a step toward mastering them. We ask ourselves, "What can I learn from this particular difficulty? What can I gain from it? This experience is not pleasant, I admit, but what can I take to repay me for its unpleasantness?" No strength of character develops without meeting trials and overcoming hardships, for character grows as muscles expand, through sweat and strain and effort. Like a piece of graceful silverware, it must undergo purifying, hammering, shaping and polishing to reveal its beauty. Paradoxical as it seems, we normally give the best account of ourselves when fighting against odds and make the poorest showing when circumstances are easiest. Often that which helps us over a difficult obstacle is to have surmounted the preceding one.

The early pages of the Bible record a desperate struggle at midnight between Jacob and a heavenly antagonist. Jacob had tricked his brother, had hoodwinked his aged father and had taken advantage of his father-in-law. He was selfish and materialistic; he would stop at nothing to advance his own cause. Finally, his snide deeds caught up with him and he was locked in a deadly grapple with a celestial opponent. Pantingly he cried, "I will not let thee go until thou bless me!"

If we wrestle with our trials in the same spirit, the blessings we wring from our difficulties help to transform them. A creative attitude, demanding that our hardships bless us, transmutes them into opportunities and turns our trials into advantages. Thomas A. Edison became deaf, an affliction from which most of us cringe. Yet toward the end of his life Edison remarked to a friend that he would not have been able to achieve what he had if he had not been stricken with deafness; he would not have been able to concentrate as thoroughly and this would have limited his success. Louis Braille, blinded at the age of three, completed the Braille system of reading and writing for the blind when he was twenty, and struggled the rest of his life to have the system accepted. A few days before his death a blind girl, a brilliant pianist, told her audience: "Your applause is not for me. It belongs to a man who is dying. . . . He has not only given the blind of the world windows, but he has given them music to weep by." Braille struggled with his affliction until it blessed an untold army of sufferers, sending light into their darkness. Wilberforce of England had a twisted, shriveled body. His suffering gave him greater insight into the agonies of the unfortunate and his passionate speeches against slavery thundered through the halls of Parliament until he awakened the conscience of his country. Because Wilberforce wrestled with his own infirmity, the day came when slavery of the black man was abolished by the law of the land. The supreme example of the creative use of adversity is a Carpenter nailed to a blood-drenched cross. From the depths of suffering, Jesus of Nazareth fashioned a light which the darkness never has been able to quench, transforming that tragedy into spiritual triumph for countless millions.

The spirit in which we meet trouble makes a decisive difference in the outcome. At times the achievement of happiness hinges on the acceptance of personal trials as challenges, coupled with the determination to wrest from them whatever blessings they may have to bestow.

A third powerful aid is to demand that *our troubles call forth strength from within.* When hardships overtake us, it is a simple matter to pamper ourselves with self-pity or to grumble about the highhanded injustice of existence, but neither self-pity nor resentment does anything constructive to master our perplexities. "Man must be arched and buttressed from within, else the temple wavers to the dust," wrote Marcus Aurelius eighteen hundred years ago.[1] We fail to achieve marked success in overcoming personal difficulties until we gain the self-confidence that we are equal to them —or to any circumstance that life may fling against us. Once we have acquired a steady assurance—not bravado, but an inner certainty tempered by testing—the achievement of happiness springs into lively possibility. We gain resiliency, the ability to rebound. We are "afflicted . . . but not crushed; perplexed, but not driven to despair; . . . struck down, but not destroyed."

In viewing the motion picture, *The Best Years of Our Lives,* thousands were stirred with admiration by the accomplishments of a young man named Harold Russell. He had lost his hands in an accident in World War II, and in their place he used two steel hooks. In spite of this devastating handicap, crippling to both spirit and body, he fought his way back to an amazing triumph. Although he never had acted before, he played a leading role in the film and won two Academy awards for his superlative performance. Determined to help other handicapped people, he turned to the radio, to writing and to lecturing, using abilities that he had not realized he possessed. He wrote:

"My weakness—my handlessness—my sense of inferiority—has turned out to be my greatest strength. I didn't think so at the time it happened and I don't think I'd ever willingly lose my hands if I had it to do all over again. But having lost them, I feel perhaps I have gained many fine things I might never have had with them. . . . this seeming disaster has brought me a priceless wealth of the spirit that I am sure I could not have possessed otherwise. I have enjoyed a life that has been full and rich and rewarding, a life that has had a meaning and depth it never had before. . . .

"People frequently marvel at the things I can do with my hooks. Well, perhaps it is marvelous. But the thing I never cease to marvel at is that I am able to meet the challenge of utter disaster and master it. For me, that was and is the all-important fact—that the human soul, beaten down, overwhelmed, faced by complete failure and ruin, can still rise up against unbearable odds and triumph." [2]

That is the all-important fact for each of us—that the human soul has the capacity to call forth strength from within to turn defeat into victory and disaster into personal triumph. The forward progress of the world is a record of the people who have defied difficulties to best them. They have held with Seneca that "the pressure of adversity does not affect the mind of the brave man. . . . Over all that happens it throws its own complexion, because it is more powerful than external circumstances." It is perplexing that pain should be the instrument of creativity, yet it is so. Those who have contributed most to the upward climb of humanity include courageous men and women who have refused to let defeat say the final word. Enduring hardships, they have discovered inner treasures of strength and optimism, courage and confidence. It is possible for us, through the same channels of fortitude and faith, to join the goodly company of those who have used the pressures of life to expand their powers.

In this respect, our lives resemble sailboats in a regatta. The boats do not have power to change the course of the wind, but they can trim their sails and use it to drive them on their course no matter from what point it may blow. It takes skill, intelligence, patience and perseverance, yet even against adverse winds they round the buoys and cross the finish line.

> Like the winds of the sea are the ways of fate,
> As we voyage along through life:
>   'Tis the set of a soul
>   that decides its goal,
> And not the calm or the strife.[3]

Even when the winds and tide seem running against us, we need not be disheartened. There was the cobbler Cary who, as he worked at his bench, gazed at a map of the world and prayed that he might introduce the gospel to India. But what chance had he, a poor shoemaker, ever to see his dream come true? Circumstances were against him, yet he fit himself for the task he visioned and at last his opportunity came. There was Judson of Burma, "sweating it out" in the prison of a barbaric king. How could the hand of God be in that trying experience? But he refused to let his faith weaken or his zeal die, and the door of his prison finally opened to a larger service than he had ever known. There were the heroes of every age who sharpened the cutting edge of their lives against the whetstone of adversity. Without exception, they knew the face of difficulty as that of a familiar friend. If we travel a rigorous road at present, it need not steal our happiness. We can demand of our rebuffs that they call forth our inner powers.

Thus far, in discussing how to face trouble, we have considered the aid that comes from a proper perspective, a constructive attitude and a sense of inner adequacy. A fourth strength originates in *sources outside ourselves*. A war is filled with examples, on the home front as on the battle field, of people who rise to unexpected heights when confronted by a crisis. In both World War I and World War II, there was less mental sickness in the United States than in the peace years. We would expect that, under the strain of war, people would break mentally and emotionally, but this is not true. When called to high endeavor, people responded magnificently to the challenge. Real trouble comes, and almost always we command new strength, endurance and courage to meet it. It is when no stern demands confront us that we give way under the little strains and petty annoyances.

Similar strength comes to us, too, in the performance of our duties. Perhaps we have not considered our daily responsibilities as being "a very present help in trouble," but so they may prove to be. When overtaken by difficulty, it is wise to continue to do the everyday, necessary, routine things. There are clients to see, a business to run, a job to complete or stock to feed. There are dishes to wash, a house to manage, children to care for, floors to sweep and windows to clean. When discouragement robs us of our will to perform these everyday tasks, it is important to persevere in them, nonetheless. When trouble overtakes us and opens wide the door of our heart to darkness and despair, often the way to close the portal is to refuse to falter in doing our duties. The loyal performance of ordinary tasks prevents our thoughts and energies from flowing into anxiety and fear, thus deepening the sense of despondency. The discharge of duties can rock our minds off the dead center of self and enable us to tackle our difficulties with renewed vigor. To give ourselves faithfully to our entrusted responsibilities is one of the finest methods to call forth emotional stability in the time of trouble. If these call for service to others, so much the better.

Two friends met after a considerable absence. After greeting each other warmly, one asked, "How is your wife? I remember that you were worried about her."

"Yes, I was," the other replied. "It's queer how things turn out, sometimes. One day as I reached the outskirts of a little village near our home, something went wrong with my car. I couldn't get the motor to start, so I went to the door of a little house near by to call for a mechanic. A pretty young woman opened the door and, when I told her my trouble, she asked me inside. I made my call and then she introduced me to her husband who was sitting in a chair near the window. He had been pretty badly mangled in the war, but he hadn't let it affect his courage or his smile. They were just going to have a bit of lunch, and they asked me to join them. I did and got to talking with them; they were a fine pair of young people."

"But what's that got to do with your wife?" the first man asked.

"I was just getting to that," his friend said. "When I got home after having the car fixed, I told her what had happened and how nice this couple had been to me. She wanted to meet them, so I took her over. She liked them as much as I did, and became interested in them, and has done some things to help them. And, you know, in thinking about them and their problems, she's forgotten most of her own! It's made a different woman of her."

In the midst of trouble, happiness often steals near us unexpectedly. Usually it is when we are not thinking of ourselves at all, but are looking the other way, absorbed in lending a helping hand or in doing a good job.

A final resource is *a sense of companionship with the Unseen*. It is difficult to gain ascendancy over our hardships without a third dimension in our lives. We have need of height, as well as length and breadth.

In his book, *Edward Wilson of the Antarctic*, George Seaver tells with admiration the story of Edward Wilson, the doctor who accompanied Captain Robert Falcon Scott on his ill-fated Antarctic expedition and who finally died at Scott's side. The author pictures him as the gentlest of the gentle and the bravest of the brave. Then he attempts to uncover the springs of fortitude in this remarkable man. "After all, courage alone will not take you far in the Antarctic as we knew it in its old man-hauling days. . . . It's courage, and unselfishness: and helping one another: and sound condition: and willingness to put in every ounce you have: and clean living: and good temper: and tact: and good judgment: and faith. And the greatest of these is faith, especially a faith that what you are doing is of use. It's the idea which carries men on. There, if I am not mistaken, you have Bill Wilson." [4]

Faith made the difference in the life of Dr. Wilson. It was the touchstone of his fortitude. Of Wilson's death, Captain Scott wrote, "His mind is peaceful with the satisfaction of his faith in regarding himself as part of the great scheme of the Almighty." A sustaining trust at the core of his character made it possible for him to face the worst without flinching.

When Pastor Martin Niemoeller was in the United States after World War II, I had the privilege of interviewing him for a radio audience. Dr. Niemoeller had defied Hitler when the dictator tried to bend the German Church to his will. He became the spearhead of the Confessional Church movement and, as Hitler's personal prisoner, spent three years in solitary confinement in two concentration camps, one of them being the infamous prison at Dachau. "How did you endure three years of solitary confinement?" I asked. "Many men would have cracked under such an ordeal."

Dr. Niemoeller smiled and replied, "A man doesn't know what he can stand until he is put to the test."

That is true, of course, but I felt that there was a deeper source of this man's fortitude. Somewhere I had read that the Bible had been of much comfort to him and I inquired if this were true.

"Yes," he answered, "it was a great comfort. It seemed to be written for men in prison!"

That also was true; in fact, much of the New Testament was written *by* men in prison. But still I was not satisfied as to the basis of his spiritual power.

Later in the interview I asked him about his call to the ministry. He had been a U-boat commander in World War I. I inquired if some experience during his U-boat days had guided him into the Gospel ministry.

"No," he said, "not especially. I tried several occupations after the war, as a matter of fact. Then it came over me that I should dedicate my life to the Christian ministry."

"The Lord laid His hand on you, so to speak," I suggested.

Instantly he added, an earnest expression on his face, "And He has never taken it off!"

Then I knew that I had the clue for which I had been searching, the strength which had sustained him during those terrible years of solitary confinement—"He has never taken it off!" His life had a third dimension. "He endured, as seeing him who is invisible." His power came from companionship with the Unseen.

When our lives are linked with the Eternal, we have access to a power sufficient to transform our troubles into triumphs.

CHAPTER XII

Laughter Is Holy, Too

IN HIS *Memoirs of Thomas Hood*, Lord Houghton wrote: "The sense of humor is the just balance of all the faculties of man, the best security against the pride of knowledge and the conceits of imagination, the strongest inducement to submit with a wise and pious patience to the vicissitudes of human existence." A sense of humor, then, becomes an indispensable element in living a serene and happy life.

Laughter is God's soothing touch on a fevered world. A happy mind is a healthy mind, for laughter relaxes the mind from intense concentration and sets up a natural rhythm. As an archer who, coming out of battle, unstrings his taut bow so that it will not lose its vibrancy before he needs it again, so a sense of humor fits us to meet the battles of life more resourcefully. Gladness relaxes tension. Humor is one of the finest solvents for the grit of irritation in the gears of life because it helps to get rid of conflicts that really do not matter; it disposes of irrelevancies by laughing at them. It enables us to get a fresh perspective on knotty problems, a perspective which helps shift the situation into manageable proportions. George Washington, for instance, turned to humor to handle a dilemma which threatened a serious division in the early Congress. In the debate to determine the size of the Federal Army, a member introduced a resolution limiting the force to three thousand men. Washington rose to suggest an amendment which provided that no enemy ever should invade the United States with more than two thousand soldiers. Laughter immediately killed the resolution and the tension vanished.

When we develop the ability to perceive the comic elements in the experiences through which we pass, in others with whom we must cope, and especially in ourselves, we are not as likely to become upset, or to give way to anxiety and despair. A sense of humor provides a balance wheel, protecting us both from self-conceit—granting the ability not to think of ourselves more highly than we ought to think—and from an overconcern either with the world about us or with the patterns our lives are weaving. In essence, humor is an undiscourageable good will toward all existence, a warm and compassionate fellow-feeling flowing out to all humankind. Laughter has power to lift the spirit, for it can transform even tears into lenses through which to see life more clearly, and can brighten black horizons with the light of hope. This is what Robert Louis Stevenson must have meant when he wrote, "That people should laugh is a better preparation for life than many other things higher and better sounding in the world's ear."

To be able to laugh at ourselves is a sign of maturity; it proves the ability to see ourselves objectively and without prejudice. We do not take ourselves with deadly seriousness, as if the fate of the world hinged on our decisions and actions. Healthy-mindedness consists in relating ourselves sanely with the universe, not in centering the universe in ourselves. Laughter helps to erase self-pity, pride and pompousness. To see in ourselves that which is comical or incongruous and to enjoy what we see as if it were in someone else reveals emotional steadiness. If we cannot do so, but, like children, resent laughter which may be leveled against us—a child interprets being laughed at as ridicule and deeply resents it—it is obvious that we have not attained full emotional stature. But if we can chuckle at our silly mistakes and petty actions, it is evident that we are superior to them. Possibly we may tell ourselves that, although our intelligence may come from our ancestors, we cannot blame our forebears for our foolish mistakes; we must manufacture them ourselves in unguarded moments! We have the reassurance that we need not be *that* ridiculous. These absurd antics and stupid errors do not represent the real *us*. We then can shrug them off for what they are—a part of being human. Laughter can restore a sense of sanity which makes us free to laugh at anything, even ourselves. When we discover the ability to do so, we have made realistic headway in handling our personal problems.

Moreover, a sense of humor not only acts as an armor against hurts and stings, but also wins the respect and friendship of others. The popular entertainment star, Jimmy Durante, describes how he learned this valuable lesson from a boyhood experience. His mother dressed him one Sunday in a Buster Brown suit with a large flowing collar. As he slunk self-consciously along the street, he knew how the boys of the gang would jeer if they saw him, and he feared their ridicule. Then he caught sight of himself in a store window and started to laugh. As he continued to laugh, some of the gang came along; it puzzled them why he failed to run away. "Listen, you," said one of them, "what's so funny?"

He pointed to his reflection in the window and said, "Look! A guy dressed like a sissy, with a face like a horse!" Soon they were laughing, too—with him.

It dawned on him that as long as he could laugh, he was safe from the world; later he learned that laughter kept him safe from himself, also. "All of us have schnozzles—are ridiculous in one way or another, if not in our faces, then in our characters, minds or habits. When we admit our schnozzles, instead of defending them, we begin to laugh, and the world laughs with us."

Laughter has the power to lift the spirits of others, as well as to win them to our side. The chain reaction of emotional tone expands more rapidly and surely than most of us realize; let one or two people in a crowd give way to panic or fear and the emotion spreads like wildfire. A cartoon strip depicted the president of a company reprimanding the superintendent in an angry mood. The superintendent criticized the foreman who, in turn, took it out on a worker. The laborer snarled at those working with him, then went home and snapped at his wife. The wife scolded her little boy— and the boy kicked the dog! The situation is not as far-fetched as we may think. What if the president had started a chain reaction of good will and friendliness? Sunniness and laughter are infectious, and it is not necessary to be the head of the company to start the contagion.

No matter how drab or humdrum our daily doings may seem, it adds pleasure to be on the alert for whatever may elicit from us a chuckle or a smile. We can make up our minds to be attracted and amused, instead of reacting only to that which is morose and disheartening. It proves our confidence in life when we respond to it with unaffected laughter. Frustrations, atom bombs, threats of war, monotony and grief are not amusing, to be sure. If we believed that such baleful forces are to have the final inning, we would have reason never to smile again. From the perspective of a saving sense of humor, rooted as it is in hope and inner faith, we are convinced that they are not permanent. They are but a log jam in the current of life, locked in the stream by fear, ignorance and misfortune. Some day the dynamic forces of goodness will blast the key logs free and the jam will break; a brighter future lies ahead. When such a conviction upholds us, life retains a thrilling and zestful appeal, even when marred by limitations and adversity.

One of the forces which should make for joy and sincere laughter is placed in the ranks of somberness all too often; namely, religion. My grandmother, who had scant tolerance for lugubriousness in any form, used to describe dolorous people as having faces long enough to drink buttermilk out of a churn. Unfortunately, there are too many pious people who underscore the fitness of the description. Even worse, they believe that this is the proper attitude to take toward their faith; they assume that religion *is* a matter of solemnity and gloom. Cruden, whose scholarly labors produced the concordance that graces many ministerial libraries, described humor thus: "To laugh is to be merry in a sinful manner." That was in 1769, but many moderns take the same view. To be good means to be solemn. To be religious means to repress joy.

When religion is considered synonymous with gloom, it loses immeasurable influence. Through the years spiritual leaders have so stressed the distinction between "worldly" and "sacred," placing everyday life apart from religion, that the average man now assumes that religion has little to do with the world. Albert Schweitzer, in a discerning criticism of the theology of Karl Barth, comments on this fact. "Karl Barth is a truly religious personality, and in his sermons there is much profound religion. But the terrible thing is that he dares to preach that religion is turned aside from the world and in so doing expresses what the spirit of the age is feeling." [1] As a result, "the spirit of the age" considers that religion is something somber, unrealistic and otherworldly, with little or no pertinence to workaday affairs.

Yet this is a false distinction, for religion at its best permeates all of life. All of life is religious, for all of its components are a part of God's purpose and plan. God ordained laughter as well as tears, joy as fully as sorrow, fun as surely as serious endeavor. In the house of religion, it is a mistake to place gloom in the seat of honor and to relegate good cheer to the kitchen—or to the backyard. Laughter is holy, too!

When we take all of life as from God's hand, religion ceases to be a sanctimonious segment from which we have squeezed most of the juices of joy. "Bless the Lord, O my soul, and forget not all his benefits," cried the Psalmist. When we perceive that God does not place a premium on pursed lips, foreboding visages and sad hearts, a lightness and gaiety can enter our lives to clothe religion with a deeper personal satisfaction and make us more attractive, better-balanced people. As E. Stanley Jones remarked, many gloomy personalities think that they are wearing martyr's crowns when in reality they wear only dunce caps. Oliver Wendell Holmes confessed that if the preachers of his day had not looked and acted like undertakers, probably he would have been a clergyman. In defense of morticians, they have changed, too!

Where did the idea originate that religion is morose? Why did the conviction take root that gladness is profane and gloom holy? The strain of somberness runs through religion from its outset, to be sure, possibly because religion deals with the heartbreaks of life as well as with its raptures. But in the true expression of religion, even at the darkest moments, the note of joy has soared triumphantly above the clouds of calamity and suffering. As John Donne wrote over four hundred years ago, "Religion is not a melancholy, the spirit of God is not a dampe."

Asceticism long was believed to have special religious significance. The word "ascetic" comes from the Greek *askesis,* which originally referred to the training of athletes and later to the discipline for piety and religious virtue by curbing or denying the desires of the flesh. In the early Christian

Church, under the influence of the Greek writers and of certain Jewish attitudes, there arose an increased emphasis on asceticism until, in the second century, it was commonly held that ascetic denial and mortification of the body was a higher form of religious expression than the practice of the positive Christian virtues.

Certain incidents and legends reveal, however, that even asceticism could not squeeze all humor out of religion. One amusing legend relates that St. Thomas Aquinas, having lingered too long at his writing, was late for vespers. As he hurried to his prayers, he passed a statue of the Blessed Virgin, who said to him reproachfully, "Thomas, thou art late." "Mary," he replied, "this is the hour of silence!"

In the United States, the strong hands of Puritanism shaped and directed religious expression. Standing first for an ecclesiastical ideal, the Puritans developed an intense preoccupation with moral issues which, coupled with an equally intense belief in original sin, led to stern self-discipline in morals and religion. Puritanism made many constructive contributions to the life and character of America, including its stress on personal responsibility and the performance of duty, the supremacy of conscience, the separation of Church and State, and the promotion of constitutional liberty, all of which helped lay the foundation for much of the nation's later industrial and political progress. Religiously, however, it devoted itself so passionately to the God of Justice that it almost overlooked the God of Love. It was stern business to overcome "the world, the flesh and the devil"; so stern that it left little room for laughter and gaiety. Yet even though their devotion to God was a serious affair, the Puritans found a somber joy in their faith.

Their spiritual heirs lost the joy and retained the repression. God became the incarnate "Thou Shalt Not." He was the unrelenting Judge who noted each human error and waited gloatingly to punish each transgression. Misery became the thermometer of holiness. In a sense, the decision for any action was easy; if it were a pleasant thing to do, it was wrong. If it were fun, it was wicked. God always demanded that men and women do those things which they did not want to do. The more somber and distasteful the action, the more holy it was likely to be.

Many intelligent and morally upright people, although they still held respect for the Church, associated religion with a life of repression, negation and gloom. Religion thus became for them not wings but a weight, not a strength but a stumbling block. In increasing numbers, they divorced themselves from vital association with the Church.

Their reaction was due largely to a misunderstanding of the true nature of religion. At its fullest and finest, religion is replete with fundamental joy. It puts songs on the lips, hope in the heart and spring in the step. Laughter is holy, too!

Consider the life of the One who is the source and foundation of the Christian faith. A common conception of him is that of "a man of sorrows and acquainted with grief." To be sure, he knew grief and bore sorrows, but gloom is not the hallmark of his personality. A careful study of the Gospels reveals that we malign him when we think of him as so borne down with melancholy that he never smiled.

The artists of earlier centuries have much to do with the conception of Jesus as consumed in a stern cosmic struggle against agony and death. They painted a black background before which the events of his life took shape. Theologically and artistically they were attracted by the dramatic qualities of his suffering, death and resurrection. Therefore, they concentrated their imaginations and skills on the agony in the garden, the cruel trial, the Via Dolorosa, the inhuman treatment on the cross, the entombment and the resurrection. Of all these events, the resurrection alone touched the note of joy, but in essence even its cheer was unearthly and ethereal.

The poets and hymn writers also bear their share of the responsibility. As with the artists, laughter and joy held less dramatic appeal for them than struggle and agony. They, too, pictured religion largely in terms of suffering and gloom. Add the effects of our own imaginations to the impressions created by the poets, hymn writers and artists, and the result becomes a distorted picture of the personality of Jesus and of the religion which he founded.

There must have been a radiance about the Galilean that attracted people to him as flowers to the sun. When the "common people heard him gladly," they were entranced by no stern and sorrowful man, long-faced and solemn, filled with a venom that curdled the joy of living. They listened to one who "spoke as no man ever spoke," whose scintillating personality gave almost irresistible appeal to the profound thought which he clothed in vivid phrase and with a delicious sense of humor. He spoke of those who gagged at a gnat, yet swallowed a camel, and of those who put a lamp under the bed instead of on a lampstand. He called attention to the man who could not attend a feast because he had wedded a wife; married men in the crowd must have grinned ruefully. With gentle irony he gave advice on removing the splinter from another's eye, first having removed the log from one's own. He founded his Church on a pun—"Peter" and "rock" come from the same Greek word. His counsel to the religious leaders on how to acquire the chief seats at the feasts is a masterpiece of witty reproof. "You greatly desire the chief places at the feasts and you hardly know how to get them," he said, in paraphrase. "Here is the method. When the guests are invited to the table, do not make the mistake of rushing to claim the conspicuous places. That is the wrong technique. The chances are that the host will enter with another person on his arm and will ask you to move. You then must retreat to the foot of the table, covered with embarrassment. Be smart and take the unimportant seats first. When the host comes in and sees you sitting at the foot of the table he will say, 'Oh, this will never do; come up higher.' Then you will have the privilege of moving up before the envious eyes of the whole company!"

As a matter of fact, Jesus' own joyous behavior was a scandal to his enemies. An amazing amount of space in the Gospels is allotted to instances where Jesus attends a party or a feast. The religious conservatives of his day found difficulty in reconciling these actions with their staid ideas of religion. "He eats with publicans and sinners," they accused him. Since "a man is known by the company he keeps," they tarred him with the same stick, a stick not stained with solemnity or smelling of sanctity!

Moreover, would the "publicans and sinners" have invited Jesus to their banquets if he had been the morose kill-joy that popular imagination often pictures him? Such persons do not seek out gloomy company for the sake of appearing religious. The fact that they invited him to dine with them speaks eloquently of the radiant personality of the Master. To the charge that he consorted with such, he replied that it was they who needed what he had to give—new life and fresh gladness. "It is not the well who have need of the physician, but the ill," he told his tormentors. The satisfaction that he found in bringing back lost men and women to the true quality of life was the kind of gladness the shepherd experienced when he rescued a lost sheep, the quality of happiness a woman enjoys who loses a precious coin and finds it again, or the joy a father feels when a prodigal son comes home.

Pious people were aghast because Jesus held the practice of fasting in such loose regard. A Pharisee fasted two days each week as a recognized feature of his faith. Jesus was forced to defend the joyful conduct and the lack of fasting among his disciples. "How can the children of the bride-chamber fast when the bridegroom is with them?" he asked. In symbolizing himself as a bridegroom, he seized on a moment of supreme human joy. He and his disciples were as happy as a bridal party, he declared, and therefore solemnity and fasting had no place in their lives. It was a clever analogy for, according to the ancient Jewish law, a bridal party was exempt from obeying the injunction to fast.

Even after he was parted from them, a spirit of joy seemed to envelop the disciples. Soon persecutions broke out, scattering the little band of believers like seeds before a storm. One of those responsible for the persecution was Saul of Tarsus, a grim, bitter, tormented man. One day on the road to Damascus, as he was pursuing some of the followers of the Way who had fled (it was later, at Antioch, that they were first called Christians), he suddenly met the Risen Lord and his torment disappeared. In his subsequent messages to the little churches he had founded across the ancient world, his sentences were punctuated with gladness, even when he wrote from prison. "For the kingdom of God," he informed the church at Rome, "is . . . righteousness, and peace and joy." To the church at Philippi he wrote, "Rejoice, and again I say, rejoice." "Love," he told those at Corinth, "rejoices not in iniquity, but rejoices in the truth." He reminded the faithful in Galatia, "The fruit of the spirit is love, joy, peace." A sunlit chord of joy runs through all he wrote. Where is its source, except in the gay, infectious spirit of the Master?

As Leslie Weatherhead has noted, when we clear away the accumulated assumptions of the centuries, the picture we get of the founder of the Christian faith is that of a radiant, laughter-loving friend, adored by children and magnetic in his appeal to all except those blinded by bias, self-interest, or importance. Like a subway train that, passing through the station, sets the little papers dancing after it between the tracks, so one could tell where Jesus had been by the lives that danced behind him. What a pity that we have allowed this radiance to escape! It is unfortunate that, when we think of religion, we think of repression and lack of joy. For emotional health and for the sake of happiness it is essential to disabuse ourselves of the notion that the religious life is filled with negations and that it puts a premium on gloom. Laughter is holy, too!

When we form the happy habit of facing each day with humor and appreciation, life becomes full and entrancing. And we need not concern ourselves as to whether or not others will find us interesting. Those who are entertained by life never fail to be entertaining. This is a bonus life pays to those who learn that laughter, too, is a gift from God.

CHAPTER XIII

The Conquest of Suffering

THE problem of suffering haunts mankind. There is not a household on which its shadow does not fall, and not a life which fails to feel its touch. To live is to suffer. It is impossible to achieve any satisfying depth of happiness without first coming to grips realistically with the problem of pain.

An ancient Greek legend [1] tells of a woman who came to the River Styx to be ferried across to the land of departed spirits. The ferryman, Charon, informs her that it is her privilege to drink of the waters of Lethe and thus to forget the life that she is leaving. Eagerly she asks, "Then I can drink and forget all my suffering?"

"Yes," he says, "and also you will forget all your joys."

"I will forget all my failures?"

"And all your triumphs."

She inquires, "I will forget how I have been hated?"

"Yes," he answers, "and you will forget how much you have been loved."

In the end, the woman leaves the draught untasted, choosing to retain the memory of life's pains, sorrows and failures rather than to forget its joys, its triumphs and its loves.

We shrink from pain. Yet, even as we endure it, we sense that there are other values superior to freedom from agony. Given the opportunity, like the woman in the legend, to escape suffering at the cost of achievement, joy and love, would we choose differently?

If, then, there are human values more precious than freedom from pain, there is the possibility of meeting the problem of suffering successfully. A young Carpenter was bold
enough to live counter to the beliefs of his time and to strip
aside pretense and sham. He dared to go against the religious
respectability of the leaders of his day and they broke him
on a cross. In the agony of that dark moment he cried aloud
—and his cry echoes that of suffering humanity through all
the ages—"My God, my God, why . . .?"

Yet before he died he found the answer to his agonized
cry and died in a spirit of complete trust. "Father, into thy
hands I commend my spirit." I must confess that I have no
easy answer to the problem of pain and hold no brief for the
suffering in the world. The "Why?" wrung from the Galilean's lips is as poignant now as then. Our problem is to find
a like transcendence over the dark seas of suffering.

Oscar Wilde, gifted but pitiable, once declared that there
was enough suffering in a single London lane to deny the
existence of God. That is one answer to the question of suffering, simply that there is no answer since there is no God.
But it is oversimple and there is no comfort in it. It accounts
for one agony by a deeper one and fails to remove the first.

In the same vein, the philosopher Hume wrote, "Were a
stranger to drop suddenly into this world, I would show him,
as a specimen of its ills, a hospital full of diseases, a prison
crowded with malefactors and debtors, a field of battle
strewn with carcasses, a fleet floundering in the ocean, and
a nation languishing under tyranny, famine and pestilence."

During a touching scene in Eugene O'Neill's play, *All
God's Children Got Wings*,[2] one character asks another,
"Will God forgive me?"

"Maybe he can forgive you for what you have done to
me," the second replies, "and maybe he can forgive me for

what I've done to you, but I don't see how God can forgive himself."

The second speaker has touched a universal question. With all the misery which exists in the world, how can God forgive Himself? Is God helpless before the ruthless surge of evil? Or is there a creative Purpose which can encompass pain and turn it to victorious ends? What answer can we find to allow us to live with inner steadiness and to achieve a satisfying allotment of happiness? Is it foolish to affirm that God *is* and that God is love? Can we discover a power sufficient to sustain us when we suffer and save us from dismay? What steadiness can our souls command when we confront human agony?

The first step is *to determine why pain comes.* Why do heartbreak and misery haunt our world and cast dark shadows across our lives? On occasion I hear someone cry in anguish of soul, "What terrible thing have I done that God should punish me so?" The answer is—*nothing!* Suffering, except through the universal laws of cause and effect, does not come as punishment. Once and for all, we should rid ourselves of the thought that the Creator of life sends pain as punishment. The idea is not consistent with the love of God. Yet a rich harvest can ripen from the dark seeds of pain. Not as punishment, but *in order that we may grow,* God has placed us in a world where there is the possibility of suffering.

Your child pleads with you for a pair of ice skates. There is nothing in the world your child wants more at the moment than a pair of skates! Now you face a dilemma. Should you buy the skates for your child, thus granting him the opportunity to develop co-ordination, grace, rhythm and the sense of achievement which come through the mastery of skating? Or should you protect your child from physical harm by refusing to give him the skates, thus sparing him the bumps, bruises and even the broken bones which may result in learning to skate? When you refuse to buy the skates for your child you protect him from pain, but you deny him the possibilities of development and personal satisfaction in this area of achievement. In order to grow he must risk suffering.

God faced a similar dilemma. He confronted the choice of building a safe world filled with moral weaklings, or of creating a world in which there was the possibility of suffering and likewise the possibility of growth in character and moral strength. Without the possibility of pain there could be no opportunity for development, no mastery through struggle, for men would be but automatons.

Charles Péguy faces this problem in the poem "Freedom." He causes God to say:

. . . . they must work out their salvation for themselves.
   That is the rule.
It allows no exception. Otherwise it would not be interesting. They would not be men.
Now I want them to be manly, to be men, and to win by themselves
Their spurs of knighthood.
                    • • • •
Such is the mystery of man's freedom, says God.
And the mystery of my government towards him and towards his freedom.
If I hold him up too much, he is no longer free
And if I don't hold him up sufficiently, I am endangering his salvation.
Two goods in a sense almost equally precious.
For salvation is of infinite price.
But what kind of salvation would a salvation be that was not free?
What would you call it?
We want that salvation to be acquired by himself,

Himself, man. To be procured by himself.
To come, in a sense, from himself. Such is the secret,
Such is the mystery of man's freedom.

It is well to remember that God does not *will* suffering.
The anguish of the world stems from other sources than
God's will. Much of it, for instance, is the result of the carelessness, folly and wickedness of those about us. In high
school and college days I played football. In one game I was
injured and played an entire second half of which I can
remember nothing except the play in which I was hurt.
One of my teammates had failed to carry out an assignment
and I paid the penalty for his failure. It would be incorrect,
would it not, to consider that God willed my injury that day?
A teammate had made a mistake; I suffered the consequences. That is part of the risk one takes in return for the
fierce fun of football.

Again and again in the game of life, pain or injury occurs
in much the same fashion. Someone, in carelessness, folly or
willfulness makes a mistake and an innocent person must
suffer as the result. Such suffering is inevitable as part of the
game of life, and it is wise to accept it as such.

As I wrote the words above, the telephone rang and the
voice on the line was that of a woman whom I know well, a
woman in great distress. Her husband has deteriorated rapidly into alcoholism. His actions have caused the estrange-
ment of relatives and friends, the disruption of the family
and the alienation of the children. The wife has endured
humiliation, shame and mental anguish, not the least of
which has been to see the man she loves debase himself so
completely. His alcoholism has so robbed him of his once
splendid abilities that he is no longer competent to retain
executive responsibility in the company which he helped to
develop. Much of the time he seems more beastlike than
human.

By any stretch of the imagination can it be maintained that God willed this wife to suffer through the faults of a drunken husband? Or is it nearer the truth to say that her suffering results from his folly and moral weakness? The innocent suffer with the guilty; this explains much of the pain we are forced to endure.

Suffering comes, also, *because we are human.* We are members of the family of mankind; we are intertwined for good or ill with all others throughout the world. As John Donne, the seventeenth-century poet, phrased it: "No man is an Iland, intire of it selfe; every man is a peece of the Continent, a part of the maine; if a Clod bee washed away by the Sea, Europe is the lesse, as well as if a Promontorie were; . . . any mans death diminishes me, because I am involved in Mankinde. . . ."

A house in Chicago burned to the ground. During the fire a little girl rushed into the flaming building and saved her brothers and sisters, although in rescuing them she herself was horribly burned. Her heroism won the imagination and generous heart of Chicago; gifts showered on her at the hospital and a new home was erected for her family. She sacrificed herself without hesitation to save her brothers and sisters. Her suffering came because she was a member of her family.

A young man belongs to the family called the United States of America. A war breaks out and in defense of his country he lays down his life. God did not will either the war or the young man's death. It was a terrible price to pay, but he paid it because he was part of the family.

Each of us is related to the family of humanity. We are "involved in Mankinde." Part of the suffering we undergo is the price of the privilege.

Likewise, suffering results from *willful disobedience.* A

mother warned her little boy, "John, don't play near the grating. It is dangerous to do so and you may hurt yourself." In the excitement of his game, little John forgot his mother's warning. He fell through the grating and broke his leg. At first the doctor thought that he would not be able to walk again. Carelessly, the nurse said something to this effect and was overheard by the little boy. As his mother leaned over the bed, he threw his arms around her neck, wept hot tears and said, "Mother, I know that I was wrong and I disobeyed you and that was naughty. But if I never walk again, will you still love me?"

You can imagine the answer to that tearful question. He sighed in relief. "Well, even if I don't walk again, it's going to be all right."

Little John did walk again. Note, however, that his suffering came, not because his mother willed it, but because he disobeyed. Similarly, our disobedience to the natural or moral laws, or to the laws of society or of health brings suffering to ourselves and others. God does not will such suffering. It is the result of disobedience.

Pain, we then can agree, does not come as punishment from the hands of a vengeful God. There is comfort in the thought. It reaches us as a part of the price we pay for mental, moral and spiritual development, or as the result of the folly and disobedience of ourselves and others. We are called on to endure suffering because we belong to the family of humanity.

Deeper still, the possibility of pain is part of the obligation of *living as sensitive human beings*. The higher the scale of existence ascends, the greater is the capacity for suffering. On my desk is half of a Montana moss agate. Years ago it was a solution, but under terrific pressure and temperature changes the solvent evaporated and what remained was pressed into flintlike quartz. It was so hard that, when it was cut in half, the saw was pointed with diamond dust. But through the entire process, from solution to sawing, it experienced not the slightest twinge of pain; a rock has no capacity for suffering. A crab has some, yet a crab can feast on another crab impervious to the fact that a third is feeding on it. The crab has little sensitivity and therefore almost no capacity for pain. A horse, for example, being higher in the scale of existence, has much more feeling than a crab. Yet, in the capacity for pain, the most sensitive horse cannot compare with a sensitive man or woman.

There is this compensation, however. The higher we go in the scale of values, the greater becomes the capacity for *joy* as well as for suffering. This fact must not be overlooked. Some individuals are so sensitive to color that they become physically ill when certain raw colors clash. But the person with such delicate reaction to color has a capacity for appreciation of the beauties of color which outstrips that given to the rest of us. The ear most sensitive to harmony is the ear most pained by discord. It is hard to conceive that any of us would be tempted to escape pain by choosing an animal-like or crab-like existence at the cost of the capacity for higher enjoyment.

It is possible that God could have made us not to be pained by what happens in the world about us—by slums, war or illness; or in the world near us—the tribulations of our loved ones and friends. By the same token, it would have denied the possibility to endow us with a capacity to love, to thrill to the beauty of a sunset or a Rembrandt, to appreciate the rich blessings of home and companionship, to know the quiet satisfaction of accomplishment, and to "rejoice with them that do rejoice, and weep with them that weep." The qualities which expand life and make it human—could we do without them, even at the cost of pain?

In order to adjust our lives to the fact of suffering, not only must we expect pain, but also *we must learn to accept it*. Normally we rebel against pain. We want none of it. Our passion to escape may lead to subtle and complex forms of flight. We may try to avoid pain through invalidism, as paradoxical as that may seem. In our subconscious we reason somewhat like this: "The struggle is too hard and there is too much to bear. The danger of getting hurt is too great. If I become ill, I can give up the struggle and avoid the possibility of pain." We retreat to the bed or the wheel chair. We become invalids. The doctor knows that there is nothing wrong with our bodies. Organically we are sound; the illness lies in our minds and wills. Usually we do not realize what we have done to ourselves, for the subconscious has fooled us completely.

At times we attempt to flee by giving way to self-pity. We feel sorry for ourselves and expect sympathy from others. We whine. We persuade ourselves that we are martyrs and that no one understands us. We whimper, "Nobody ever has suffered as I am suffering. No one guesses the amount of misery and pain I bear. I shall endure it nobly, in silence. Some day, when it is too late, they'll be sorry!"—and we convince ourselves!

Of course, such an attitude is foolish and deserves contempt rather than sympathy. We should avoid self-pity at all costs because of its deteriorating effect on character. The self-sorry personality gathers fears and anxieties as a burr gathers yarn. It becomes fevered with accumulated resentments. Personal experiences get sadly out of focus. In *Twelfth Night*, Olivia rightly diagnoses Malvolio's malady. "O! you are sick of self-love, Malvolio, and taste with a distempered appetite. To be generous, guiltless and of free disposition, is to take those things for bird-bolts that you deem cannon-bullets." The more we indulge in self-pity, the more

distorted seems the world around us, and the more unhappy
we become.

We also attempt to ignore suffering. By closing our hearts
and minds to the misery in the world about us, we hope
somehow to escape it—to build a personal immunity. This
attitude should not be confused with a healthy-minded objectivity that does not rule out sympathy and compassion.
Neurotically to ignore suffering does not destroy it, nor does
such a position prepare us emotionally to endure suffering
when it reaches us. It is extremely difficult to ignore pain
when we are the sufferers. An ancient jingle touches the heart
of the matter:

> There was a faith healer of Deal
> Who said, "Although pain isn't real,
> When I sit on a pin,
> And it punctures my skin,
> I don't like what I fancy I feel."

These are but a few in a long list of flights from reality.
Each one makes us less healthy, more thoroughly disliked,
and a lesser personality than we should be.

We must not flee from suffering. In fact, from the standpoint of mental health, it is dangerous to do so. When we
strive to meet pain with courage and faith, and to face it
without flinching, we are on the road to emotional acceptance and spiritual growth. The brilliant young writer, Katherine Mansfield, died when she was thirty-three years of age.
During her long struggle with illness, she wrote in her journal: "I should like this to be accepted as my confession.
There is no limit to human suffering. When one thinks: Now
I have touched the bottom of the sea, now I can go no deeper
—one does go deeper. I do not want to die without leaving a
record of my belief that suffering can be overcome, for I do
believe it. What must one do? Do not resist it. Take it. Be

overwhelmed. Accept it fully. Make it a part of life. Everything in life that we really accept undergoes a change. So suffering must become love. . . ." [3]

Thus she accepted her suffering and was not defeated by it. Who can help but admire such a spirit? If we are to emerge victorious over suffering, we must not quake before it or attempt unrealistically to evade it. Like Katherine Mansfield, we must accept it, remembering that "everything in life that we really accept undergoes a change." We must acquiesce to pain fully, no longer rebelling against it or questioning bitterly why it sought us out, but with open hearts and minds receive whatever muted messages it may bring. Then we are in a position to take the next constructive step— to *use our suffering creatively.*

Pain is a wise teacher if we have the insight to accept its wisdom. It can teach us to be grateful for the quiet, enduring blessings which hallow our lives and which otherwise we may carelessly ignore. When we examine a jewel, the merchant often places the gleaming gem on a piece of black velvet so that against the dark background the beauty of the jewel shines with a brighter luster. At times life places its jewels against the black background of suffering. When we see them thus, it should teach us a deeper appreciation of their beauty. All ease makes us selfish. All comfort makes us careless and steals from us the spirit of gratitude. When there is no cross, there is likely to be no crown.

In the Gospels, many of the beautiful pictures follow hard on the heels of some ugly thing. In the twenty-first chapter of St. Luke, for instance, Jesus outlines the grim tragedies which will befall his disciples. Then he tells them, "It shall turn to you for a testimony." In other words, Jesus seems to be saying, "These sufferings become your opportunity to witness to your faith. They are your opportunities to be strong, loving and kind. Take hold of these baleful things and turn them into something useful and upbuilding. Do not try to escape them; submit to them and transform them into something higher. Force these hardships to serve the deeper, creative purposes of your lives." Then, as if clothing his words with deeds, he hung on a cross and "was perfected in suffering."

Take the matter of friendship, for example. When all goes well and prosperously, we have many acquaintances (although we may call them friends), but when adversity strikes and the tides of success run against us, the fair-weather friends drop away. Nor do we wish for them to stay because, in our times of anguish, they cannot give us the essential answers for which we thirst. When trouble overtakes us, we desire friends on whom we can lean, people who have within themselves wells of quiet strength and stability. In an hour of anguish, when we find a friend who can enrich and sustain us from his own store of spiritual sufficiency, then we have learned what friendship can truly mean. Almost without exception, such sufficiency is purchased over the counter of suffering.

Consider the matter of citizenship. In pioneer days my great-grandparents trekked by wagon train to the western plains. They struggled, fought and suffered for the land they claimed. They endured droughts, grasshoppers, plagues and Indian uprisings. They underwent border raids and full-scale war. In the end, they owned their land and loved their country with a fierce patriotism. Their citizenship and the soil they tilled had cost them much in suffering.

The summary of a magazine survey [4] concluded with these words: "The success of communism is the result of the failure of Christians who have forgotten the revolutionary demands of their faith." The survey suggested specifically that the weakness of America's position stems from the self-satisfaction of its people, people who "assume that they are quite as virtuous as anyone can be and love their fellowmen as much as anyone should."

Having read these words, I talked with a friend who remarked, "Most of us have not suffered enough for our country; this in spite of the fact that many men have bled in battle, and many homes have known anguish and loss. Many Communists have suffered for their cause and are willing to keep on doing so. That is why communism is a threat. When we are willing to pay as great a price, the danger of communism will diminish. It takes a passion to overcome a passion."

My friend was right. A passion can be conquered only by a stronger passion. Citizenship, like faith, never shines at its brightest until it glows with the fires of testing. It, too, is "perfected in suffering."

Although we cannot escape pain, we can determine to what ends we shall use it. What happens to us is not as significant as the attitude we take toward what happens to us. In one of his sermons Harry Emerson Fosdick quoted a woman who said pityingly to a courageous girl who was undergoing severe pain, "Suffering so colors life!" In the midst of her agony the girl replied, "Yes,—and I propose to choose the color!"

The face of a woman in a hospital bed was pale and drawn, but she made no complaint. In a low voice she confided, "There was a woman in the next bed—she was such a baby! She moaned and whined and wanted sympathy. She drove the nurses almost to distraction. I am determined that I will not behave like that, no matter what I go through." She was choosing the color.

Illness can harden one man and make another gentle. The difference lies not in the illness, but in the men. Sorrow can embitter a woman, causing her to close the shutters of her house of life and darken all within. Another, like Josephine

Butler, chooses a different color. She came home late one night and her little girl, an only child, heard her enter. The child rushed excitedly from her upstairs bedroom to greet her mother, tripped, fell over the balustrade and landed on the floor at her mother's feet. When she picked up her little girl, the child was dead.

Mrs. Butler could have turned bitter, or let her grief break her. She could have grown cynical and despairing, as a lesser person might have done. Instead, she accepted her grief and *used* it. Her thoughts turned to the little orphaned girls who had no mother's love, and she determined to pour out the love she would have given to her own little girl on these love-starved children. Because she used her grief creatively, hundreds of children came to know a mother's care. Josephine Butler chose the color of her affliction.

Pain, then, can be transformed. It is not enough for us to endure suffering. Beyond endurance lies acceptance, and acceptance is complete when we use our pain creatively.

There is something more which pain and suffering can do to deepen character and lead to the achievement of happiness. When accepted completely and with a pliant spirit, *it has power to release spiritual and moral strength.* When we ask ourselves what the purpose of life is, the *raison d'être* of existence, we come to this answer: *the purpose of life is to mold character.* Then how does character develop? What forces shape it? Not comfort and ease, surely, although we need both. Not petting and pampering, for they sap moral vigor and shape weaklings. Not the pursuit of greedy, selfish aims, for these can make a person more like a beast than a man. Not self-excuse and self-pity, for something shrivels within the individual who whines his way through life. We have but to look at someone who epitomizes these weaker ways of facing existence to see the fate from which our hardships and sufferings have saved us. Character is achieved as mastery is acquired in any worthy field, through effort, discipline and testing.

John Ruskin, in one of his books on architecture, maintains that in order for a building to stand stalwart and strong there must be an element of shadow in it. The structure must contain a deep recess or a towering wall; the shadow thus cast adds strength and character to the building. The same principle applies to the house of personality. When some deep crevice of sorrow or pain exists, leading not to bitterness but to the release of inner powers, its shadow adds depth and attractiveness to personality in a manner that gentler experiences are powerless to duplicate. Personalities untouched by pain are to be pitied. "A sunshine makes a desert," the Arabs say—and all sunshine makes a life shallow.

> Only the soul that knows the mighty grief
> Can know the mighty rapture. Sorrows come
> To stretch out spaces in the heart for joy.

When we desire a wood with magnificent grain, we do not choose a soft pine from a sheltered valley. We select a sturdy hardwood tree which, twisted and tormented, has battled the elements high on a lonely skyline. The dawn shines most radiantly after the blackest night. The perfume of the rose is most poignant after the petals are crushed. In the physical world or in the personal, suffering has a strange power to release beauty and strength. All character bears affidavit of struggle.

Think of Tennyson, wringing out of his sad bereavement the inspiration to write *In Memoriam*. John Milton wrote long and arduously, but he produced his masterpieces after he was blind. Mozart composed his immortal *Requiem* in direst poverty. George Matheson became blind in his school days, but his affliction did not deter him from entering the ministry. However, he refused the love of his sweetheart because he dreaded the poverty into which, as a blind man, he might lead her. Out of the renunciation of her love and the agony of his blindness he found the spiritual resources to write:

> O Love that wilt not let me go,
> I rest my weary soul in Thee;
> I give thee back the love I owe,
> That in Thine ocean depths its flow
> May richer, fuller be.
>
> O Joy that seekest me thro' pain,
> I cannot close my heart to Thee:
> I trace the rainbow thro' the rain,
> And feel the promise is not vain
> That morn shall tearless be.[5]

Dante was a genius of spiritual insight. Where did he gain his understanding? See him as he wanders in exile through the villages of Italy. Hear the people say to one another, "There goes a man who has been in hell!" Yet Dante could not write his *Divine Comedy* until he had lost his beloved Beatrice, had been banished from his home and had suffered until deep furrows seamed his face.

Without their pain, would any of these have achieved their power?

This does not imply that suffering turns all people into saints. It does not. It is true, as we have noted, that on the cross Jesus cried, "My God, my God, why . . . ?" In the midst of their anguish, many individuals stop with the query and live the rest of their days under the shadow of that twisted question mark.

But Jesus added, "Father, into thy hands . . ." He accepted his suffering in an attitude of trust which even death could not shake, thus releasing powers of forgiveness and healing sufficient to redeem the world. What counts is not that suffering seeks us out; what means most is the response we make when it comes.

Consider the parable of the violin string. The violin string lay in the showcase, indolent and free. The master purchased it one day and strung it across the bridge of his violin; it was dull and inert, and gave no music to his touch. He tightened the string, straining it to the breaking point, until it was in key. Then, under the master's bow, it vibrated into life and burst into glorious song.

We are that violin string stretched across the bridge of existence. Life strains us to the breaking point; we cry aloud in confusion and pain. But, when we accept the suffering aright, it is only that the Master of life may sweep his bow across our spirits and set free our song.

CHAPTER XIV

Religion, Health and Happiness

AT LEAST one half of the civilized human race is emotionally ill. A summary of industrial and army records reveals that 80 per cent of the population of the United States—an astonishing figure—needs the services of a psychiatrist. According to the National Association for Mental Health, one out of every twelve children born in the United States will spend some time in a mental hospital. Emotional and mental disturbances, more than all other diseases put together, are responsible for the hospitalization of the American people. Even more alarming is the estimate which conservative doctors make that from 30 to 50 per cent of their office patients complain of symptoms that have no physical basis. One cannot say that these people are not ill; they are. Yet there are no physical reasons why they should be.

When Forain, the French artist, was an aged man he became critically ill. Several specialists examined him. The heart specialist declared that his heart was in excellent condition; the lung specialist found nothing wrong with the lungs; the kidney specialist discovered no fault with his kidneys. The aged artist interrupted their consultation to remark: "Gentlemen, it seems from what you say that I am dying in perfect health."

It is grimly true in some instances. People do die in perfect health. Their physicians declare that they have no cause to die. Some medical men go so far as to affirm that people, except for old age and accidents, even select the time of their demise. This is not an overstatement, as numerous case histories reveal. Sigmund Freud maintained that there are two main biological forces at work within the individual: the life instinct and the death instinct. The "will to die" is as real as the "will to live," and when it gains ascendancy, it actually can destroy life.

Man is a complex, mysterious unity. He is more than body. His body is the instrument of mind and soul, and is affected by their state of health, or lack of it. There is a strong interrelatedness between body, mind and soul; one influences the others for good or ill. Today physicians emphasize this fact, insisting that when one part is sick, all is sick. Through the study of psychosomatic medicine there is a growing conception of the powerful effect which the emotions exert. Doctors at the Mayo Clinic, for instance, have stated that they can treat effectively only 25 per cent of their cases with the scientific instruments and modern medicines at their disposal. The other 75 per cent, they declare, are patients who are sending the sickness of their minds into their bodies. Before the doctors can cope successfully with the illness of the body, they first must minister to mind and soul.

Some years ago, Dr. Harold Wolff had a young patient whose throat was badly burned by drinking boiling hot soup. The scar tissue closed his esophagus and he could not swallow. In order to feed him, the doctor made an opening into his stomach through which he placed food. Through this opening Dr. Wolff was able to observe the effects of the emotions on the walls of the stomach. When the patient was resentful or aggravated, the stomach walls became rouged with blood. When he was depressed, anxious or fearful, they turned pale. When he was angry, the walls became a fiery red. In this unique way, the doctor was able to satisfy himself that the emotions have a marked effect on the bodily processes.

Even animals can become neurotic through emotional disturbance, as Dr. H. S. Liddell proved through his experiments with sheep. Sheep are not nervous animals; hence they are good subjects for this type of experiment.

Dr. Liddell placed his sheep in a laboratory where they had every comfort, except for a single distraction. In the laboratory he placed a metronome, such as one uses when learning to play the piano. The doctor set it at fifty beats per minute and let it run continuously. After the sheep became accustomed to the beat of fifty per minute, the doctor stepped up the rate to one hundred twenty beats per minute at feeding time. Soon, when the sheep heard the metronome speed up, they would rush to the feed boxes. It was not necessary for them to smell food, see someone coming, or hear the rattle of pans; the speeded metronome was all the signal they required.

After the habit was established, Dr. Liddell gradually increased the normal rate throughout the day from fifty to eighty, then ninety, and finally to one hundred beats per minute. The sheep could not distinguish between one hundred beats per minute, which represented the norm, and one hundred twenty beats at feeding time, so they rushed back and forth to their feed boxes, completely bewildered. As a result, they developed a case of nerves. They reacted as humans do! They became disgruntled and quarreled with one another, their heartbeats were fast and irregular, their bodily functions were upset, and they became sulky and refused to eat. They could not relax and go to sleep at night. Perhaps they counted men!

Dr. Liddell then put the sheep in pasture to graze. In time they recovered, but it took some of the sheep a year to become normal. When the doctor returned them to the laboratory, where again they heard the metronome, they became tense and nervous, and began to tremble. Some of them needed only to enter; the familiar sights and odors revived the nervous symptoms.

If distraught emotions thus can affect sheep, how much stronger is their impact on human beings! Resentment, rage, tension, fear and anxiety affect the body and, if they become chronic, can cause crippling illness. Such emotions as joy, enthusiasm and love, on the other hand, are health-giving and stimulating; they enrich life with a vitality and tone that it cannot have otherwise. They make it sturdier and more serene. Thus biology joins religion in declaring that love is better than hate, joy more healthful than rage, and an outgoing self superior to self-centeredness. To live happily, an understanding of the interrelatedness of religion, health and emotion is important.

First of all, religion helps *by giving a foundation of security and meaning which eases tension and anxiety*. Such a foundation is essential to vigorous mental health. If we are jittery or afraid, if we are uncertain of life's meaning or of the ideals for which we stand, if we are anxious about what the future holds, or if we have no *invisible* means of support (as has been said of the atheist), such insecurity attacks our emotions with disastrous consequences. In a famous and often quoted statement, Dr. C. G. Jung declared that each of his patients past thirty-five years of age had fallen ill because he had lost a religious outlook on life—if he had had one—and that none was healed who failed to regain a religious faith. "Side by side with the decline of religious life, the neuroses grow noticeably more frequent," he adds.

Each of us needs a sense of security; we cannot live adequately, let alone happily, without it. Some of us realize no need for inner resources. Life flows pleasantly for us—our financial resources are more than adequate, our position is assured, our family has a good record, and the future seems bright. When we consider it at all, we wonder idly what need we have for spiritual resources.

In reality our position is precarious, for we are at the mercy of what can happen to us. We resemble the hayricks one sees in the fields of Europe, supports on which the hay is allowed to dry. Let our supporting framework give way and we fall to the earth in a heap—we have nothing within to prop us up. Many things can happen to cause the external framework to totter. Death may strike; illness or accident may leave us handicapped; economic storms may sweep away financial security; disgrace to someone in the family may shame us; or we may be thrown into a new and bewildering environment—an army camp, for instance, or a strange city—which overnight filches from us the habitual traditions and social restraints on which we have depended for moral support, leaving us the prey of our own inner weaknesses. We face panic and disintegration; the resulting confusion may precipitate a flight into illness. At best, the tensions and fears which torment us may disrupt our health. To live happily we must find a deeper basis of security than that of external well-being.

Add to this a growing fear of personal inadequacy, likely to arise in the absence of inner supports. We remember past failures and former defeats, and become pessimistic about our powers. We are face to face with a hard problem, and are doubtful of our ability to solve it; we are confronted with a difficult job, and tell ourselves that we cannot handle it; we meet hardship or trouble, and conclude that we cannot stand it. We are like a football team with a weak bench; when we battle a powerful opponent, we have no strong reserves to throw into the game. The strain and tension of such continual insecurity is disastrous to mental and physical health.

Moreover, the regard which we hold for ourselves and others increases or retards the forces which augment mental health. Do we see ourselves and those with us in the bundle of humanity as insects clinging for a few uneasy moments to the epidermis of a minor planet—or as children of God? To which lasting qualities can we give our earnest allegiance— or do any values have enduring worth? How do we meet frustration, suffering and death? What convictions have we as to the ultimate meaning of things? The answers to such questions profoundly affect the emotional tone of our lives and subsequently our physical well-being.

We feel healthy and happy when the goals we have selected seem worth attaining and when we are capable of pursuing them. When filled with purpose and satisfaction, we feel no sense of ill health even from grave physical handicaps. Dr. Richard C. Cabot, of the Harvard Medical School, tells of an autopsy performed on a man sixty-five years of age who had been killed in an automobile accident. The man's widow said that her husband had been vigorous and healthy; he was never sick and he never used medicine. Yet the autopsy revealed that the man was suffering from four different diseases, any one of which was capable of killing him! He had cirrhosis of the liver, chronic kidney trouble, hardening of the arteries, and a tubercular infection in one lung. In spite of these afflictions, he had lived in vigorous health until the accident had ended his life. The amazing powers of the body to resist disease had strong bearing, of course. But even more important, life was so thrilling and compelling that his zest carried him past the invasions of physical illness; he was so absorbed and one-directional that fear and illness could gain no power over him.

When we are confused and uncertain, at loggerheads within, and no longer feel adequate to the demands of existence, the likelihood of illness increases. Dr. Gotthard Booth wrote, "As far as can be predicted from the growing experience of psychosomatic medicine and psychiatry, it seems likely that eventually all illness may be understood as a meaningful expression of the individual's particular problem of adjustment." [1]

At this point religion enters to buttress our sense of inner adequacy, and to lift our eyes from ourselves "unto the hills, from whence cometh my help." A calm, majestic, triumphant Spirit surrounds us; God's power is available for our personal needs. Such a conviction gives release from the devastating emotions which tear life apart. Josiah Royce, the philosopher, has defined religious faith as "the discovery of a Reality that enables one to face anything that can happen to one in the universe." Religion releases us from carrying Atlaslike the weight of the world by ourselves; God shares the responsibility. An invigorating confidence courses through our lives with healing and power. Our religious conviction assures us that we need not be tense and anxious. We are not orphans in the universe. All appearances to the contrary, the world in which we live is not a madman's nightmare; it is a Father's house and a loving Hand holds control. With such inner assurance, we bend before the howling gales of existence, but do not snap; we are perplexed, but not driven to despair; we are afflicted, but do not cave in. John Oxenham wrote:

> Not for one single day
> Can I discern my way,
> But this I surely know,—
> Who gives the day,
> Will show the way,
> So I securely go.

When the boundless power of God flows through the channels of our spirits with peace, joy and renewal, it purges the poisons of fear and uncertainty, and vitalizes our lives with health.

A second contribution of religion is *to encourage the positive emotional responses that build health*. We already have noted the marked effects that emotion can register in the body. For the purpose of illustration, let us compare the cells in the body to the men below deck in a battleship—the firemen, machinists and various seamen. They cannot see what is happening; their contact with the outer world is through the messages from the bridge. The report reaches them that all is well—the sun is bright, the day beautiful, the sea smooth, no enemy craft are in the vicinity, and there is no danger. They work with calm efficiency; their tasks are completed easily and without strain; they are relaxed and happy.

Then the signals change. The barometer is falling and bad weather lies ahead. A typhoon is sweeping toward them. Tense and alert, they stand by their stations during the emergency. All their energies are concentrated on their tasks; they perform their duties with taut precision. When they learn from the bridge that the typhoon is dying and that the danger is lessening, they relax slightly. Finally, the storm past, they resume their normal functions, and carry out their routine assignments without strain.

Later, the signals call them to battle stations; the ship is to engage the enemy! Disciplined excitement grips the men below. They obey orders instantly and fill every action with their best effort. All their strength is co-ordinated with that of others throughout the ship toward the achievement of victory. Not until the crisis is over and the battle won do they relax.

But suppose that the captain on the bridge is filled with anxiety and imagines danger where there is none. Tense and fearful, he continually relays messages of crisis, danger and

despair to the men below. They obey his commands; they
perform the emergency duties demanded of them. Later,
learning that there has been no emergency, they are confused
and their morale suffers. Called again and again to face imaginary crises, they become jittery and demoralized. Under
the continual impact of fear-filled messages from the bridge,
they lose efficiency; their reactions become sluggish and er-
ratic, or overcharged with emotion. If the situation continues
indefinitely, they crack under the strain.

Roughly, the cells and organs of the body resemble the
seamen below deck; they obey without question the orders
sent from above. We ourselves are the captain on the bridge.
When the messages are those of cheerfulness, trust and well-
being, the "crew" works with harmonious efficiency. When
there is honest danger, they concentrate their energies to
meet it; after the peril is past, they relax again to routine
activity. But when we are tense and fearful, we are prone to
give incessant signals of alarm to the "crew" below. They try
desperately to respond to the commands. Since they have no
reasoning intelligence, they do not question whether the risk
is real or imaginary; they simply obey. Messages of anger
or resentment, for instance, send an extra supply of blood to
the walls of the stomach, as Dr. Wolff's patient demonstrated;
that is the "crew's" method of meeting a crisis. This causes
an oversecretion of gastric juice, one element of which is hydrochloric acid. Too much hydrochloric acid—more than
enough needed to digest the proteins in the food consumed—
reacts unfavorably on the walls of the stomach. In a sufficient
period of time, an ulcer results. In much the same fashion,
under the impetus of fear, an added supply of adrenalin is
pumped into the blood stream; the body needs it to combat
danger. When fear is a habitual response to an imaginary
alarm, the excessive charges of adrenalin can damage the
body processes. Much high-blood pressure can be traced to

strong emotional responses over a prolonged period of time. Recent medical experiments indicate that even laryngitis and the common cold may be due in part to the signals which we —the captain on the bridge—send to the "crew" below.

Religion helps us to replace our insecurities with creative emotions such as love, hope, confidence and good will. Knowledge of the constructive power of such emotions is not new. Marcus Aurelius, throughout his *Meditations,* insists that our lives are what our thoughts make them.[2] Spinoza wrote: "A man who desires to help others by counsel or deed will refrain from dwelling on men's faults, and will speak but sparingly of human weaknesses. But he will speak at large of man's virtue and power, and the means of perfecting the same, that thus men may endeavour joyously to live, so far as in them lies, after the commandment of reason." There is therapeutic value as well as sound religion in St. Paul's admonition: "Whatsoever things are true, whatsoever things are honest, whatsoever things are just, whatsoever things are pure, whatsoever things are lovely, whatsoever things are of good report . . . think on these things." What we hold in our hearts becomes the standard of what we can or cannot accomplish.

On his polar expeditions, Admiral Byrd was extremely careful in selecting the men who accompanied him. They were tested for health, experience, aptitude and abilities. Beyond these rigid requirements, however, was a conclusive basis of selection: could the man stand up under difficulties and still maintain a positive, hopeful attitude? Did he have the sanguine temperament that could discover reasons for hope and believe in them? *Disposition* was the crucial test. If a man thought in positive terms, if he habitually envisioned success and not failure, if faith upheld him in the midst of difficulties, his strength and optimism affected the whole company. The expedition would be stronger and more efficient because of each man's influence.

What is our disposition, the attitude which we habitually assume? Is it negative, fearful and doleful? Do we picture obstacles and defeat? Or do we meet our responsibilities with cheerfulness and courage? When illness overtakes us, are we confident that we can cope with it successfully? Some people see the dark side of every situation; they hesitate to take the optimistic view. They resemble the man who received a physical checkup and was told by his doctor to take a rest. After a protracted vacation, he returned to the doctor's office in fine physical trim, his face tanned and glowing with health. When the physician complimented him on his handsome suntan, he replied, "Yes, I suppose I look fine on the outside, but just think how pale I am underneath!"

Unfortunately, the attitude often parallels our own. We find something to worry about in every situation; if not, we worry because we do not! We think in negative terms. We picture defeat, borrow trouble, become apprehensive about our health and the future, and anticipate only the worst. We become suspicious of the motives even of those closest and dearest. Our bodily resources wage a losing battle against such destructive emotions. It takes a strong constitution indeed to withstand such continual attacks. Trouble will seek us without our aid; why raise lightning rods of apprehension to attract it?

Religious conviction helps to defeat this destructive tendency. Sickness, war, hardship, old age, frustration, loneliness, poverty and misunderstanding—we can face them all if we have spiritual peace. "The sovereign cure for worry is religious faith," wrote William James. "The turbulent billows of the fretful surface leave the deep paths of the ocean undisturbed; and to him who has a hold of vaster and more permanent realities, the vicissitudes of his personal destiny seem relatively insignificant." A confident approach to life stimulates the harmonious response of the body, mind and spirit.

When we love and enjoy people, when we feel at one with the world and at peace with God, the marvelous powers of the body for recuperation and healing are allowed to operate without check or hindrance. No longer does our inner emotional life resemble a turbulent tug of war. We are not tense with dread or apprehension. We are not choked with a sense of guilt or suppressed rage. Nothing prevents the natural powers from performing their normal functions of renewal and recovery. "A merry heart doeth good like a medicine," the writer of the book of Proverbs declares with sound logic.

Religion offers another realistic aid to mental and physical health when *it grants release from a damaging sense of guilt*. From the dawn of conscience the problem has tormented mankind: what can a man do who has done wrong? Men have committed terrible acts in atonement. They have slashed their bodies and poured out their blood; they have tortured themselves; they have given costly sacrifices, even to the extent of offering up the lives of those most loved. Women have thrown their babies to the crocodiles, giving the fruit of their bodies for the sins of their souls. They have tried unnumbered techniques of penance to ease the fire of inner guilt. There is an innate conviction in human nature that wrongdoing is not a private matter, but has universal implication; that somehow it relates to the entire scheme of things; that it requires God's forgiveness. Anyone who has wrestled with the problems afflicting the human spirit knows the reality of such torment. The American psychologist William McDougall maintains that at the root of every phobia lies a sense of guilt. When Huckleberry Finn declares that sometimes conscience "takes up more room than all the rest of a person's insides," it makes sense to us. Finding it impossible to ignore our transgression, or to forgive ourselves, we punish ourselves in many ways, convinced that we must suffer for our misdeeds. The punishment often is harsh; as Henry David Thoreau has said, "Public opinion is a weak tyrant compared with our private opinion." Feelings of remorse cannot be sloughed off as mere morbidity, or handled as a matter of self-forgiveness. The finer the texture of our personality, the more guilt tortures us, and the more restless, tense and apprehensive we become.

Shakespeare dealt with the problem in some of his greatest dramas. Macbeth watches his wife, crazed by guilt, as in her troubled sleep she strives to wash from her hands the blood of the murdered Duncan, blood which to her frenzied mind still stains them. Then, in troubled spirit, he asks the doctor:

> Canst thou not minister to a mind diseas'd,
> Pluck from the memory a rooted sorrow,
> Raze out the written troubles of the brain,
> And with some sweet oblivious antidote
> Cleanse the stuff'd bosom of that perilous stuff
> Which weighs upon the heart?

The physician answers:

> Therein the patient must minister to himself.

The doctor's answer is only partially correct. Under a deep sense of guilt, with power to cause such extreme mental suffering as to drive us into psychosomatic illness—which means that the mind, no longer able to cope successfully with the problem, has transferred its torment to the body—we attempt many expedients to escape it. We blame our guilt on someone else. We try to rationalize it; we are "justified" in doing what we did, or were forced into it. We tell ourselves that others do much worse things. We project our guilt, seeing in those about us the wrongdoing of which we are guilty. We condemn most sternly the shortcomings to which we ourselves are prone. These and other expedients do little to ease our sense of guilt, however, especially if we have had a religious upbringing. Dr. Jung has written: "There appears to be a conscience in mankind which severely punishes the man who does not somehow and at some time, at whatever cost to his pride, cease to defend and assert himself, and instead confess himself fallible and human. Until he can do this an impenetrable wall shuts him out from the living experience of feeling himself a man among men."

Confession, as Dr. Jung points out, has constructive value in release from a sense of guilt. We may confess our wrongdoing to the one whom we have harmed, to a friend or counselor, or to one who stands as a symbol of God—to pastor, priest or rabbi. It may help to write a confession of wrongdoing, even if we destroy the record later, for writing causes us to put our feelings of guilt into concrete form. It also gets them out into the open. William James talks of "exteriorizing our rottenness" and heartily recommends such procedure. We may try restitution; that is, we attempt to make up for the harm we have done through reparation and apology. Yet, in spite of all such efforts, a sense of guilt still troubles us; something must thrust in at a deeper level to "put the fire out of our own bosom," as John Wesley phrased it expressively. As long as we refuse to admit our wrongdoing and hold the pathetic hope that somehow we can get ourselves together so that our trouble will turn out all right, there is no chance to remove our sense of guilt permanently. To cling stubbornly to such a conviction reveals a lack of understanding of our inner natures. Alcoholics Anonymous has discovered that it is unable to help those caught in the web of alcoholism until they give up the idea completely that they are strong enough to aid themselves. They must be willing to turn themselves over to a greater Power. Then—but not until then—the reconstruction of personality can begin.

We cannot find complete deliverance from the burden of our wrongdoings until, admitting our personal limitations, we are willing earnestly to seek and to accept divine forgiveness. Then God can do for us what we cannot do for our-selves. Since He alone was great enough to create us, He alone is able to *re-create* us into the relief, joy and wholeness of true forgiveness. It is hard to overestimate the therapeutic value of such a restored relationship. "Blessed is he whose transgression is forgiven, whose sin is covered," exulted the Psalmist. Forgiveness grants a release from tension and emo-tional strain, a sense of liberation and gladness, an invigorat-ing renewal of energy, and a blessed sense of relaxation and peace. Anyone having undergone such an experience can never doubt its reality. We understand the sentiments of the woman who exclaimed, "I don't see how God can forgive me, but if He does, He'll never hear the end of it!"

Our feeling of gratitude becomes all the more vivid and enduring when we link it to constructive action. With every positive emotion, we fortify *impression* through *expression*. We betray the full importance of our sense of forgiveness un-less we weave it into future service.

> Let me draw you to the Great Forgiveness,
> Not as one above who stoops to save you,
> Not as one who stands aside with counsel,
> But, as he who says I, too, was poisoned
> With the flowers that sting, but now, arisen
> I am struggling up the path beside you.
> Rise, and let us face these heights together.

Accepting forgiveness for our guilt in this humble and crea-tive spirit, we turn a liability into an asset, a minus into a plus, a loss into a gain.

In one sense, we are honor bound to do nothing less, for our forgiveness is conditional. "Forgive us our debts," we pray, *"as we forgive our debtors"*—that is the condition. To win divine forgiveness, we must be willing to forgive those who have wronged us, or against whom we hold animosity.

"He is a green hand at life," said Robert Louis Stevenson, "who cannot forgive any mortal thing."

This leads to a consideration of a further function which religion performs. When it enables us to forgive those who have harmed us, *it releases curative power*. Through the impulse of religion, it becomes possible to forgive and to cease to hold rancor. The bitter burdens of hate and wounded pride melt away. We forgive—and the dam crumbles which has blocked the flow of positive, healing powers within. The glands, the nerves, the chemistry of the body work normally once more.

The sixth chapter of St. Luke tells of a multitude who came to the Man from Nazareth to be healed of their diseases. Pouring out his spiritual strength unstintingly, he brought comfort and relief. We moderns are learning anew about the healing power of faith; psychosomatic medicine is a strong ally. When people come into vital personal contact with the Great Physician, they receive power to drive out many of the tormenting spirits that bedevil our generation.

After he had relieved the sufferers, "he lifted up his eyes on his disciples" and taught them—and what he stressed is significant. The emphasis was on forgiveness, of the refusal to sit in judgment on another's failures, and of freedom from grudge-bearing. He described the spirit of love which should flow into all areas of life, not only to those of their own households, but also to their enemies—the people whom they did not like or who had treated them shamefully. The inference is that the failure to observe these fundamental spiritual truths had caused the illnesses he had healed. "A good tree cannot bring forth evil fruit," he said, "neither can a corrupt tree bring forth good fruit. . . . A good man out of the good treasurer of the heart bringeth forth good things: and an evil man out of the evil treasure bringeth forth evil things."

If it were true in ancient days that an unloving, unforgiving spirit could cause broken health, under our modern tensions it is emphatically so. A requisite for health of mind and body is to let go our petty hatreds. We should lay them on the altar of forgiveness, together with all the tensions, troubles and unhappiness they cause. Having cleansed our hearts and having replaced animosity with a spirit of compassion, spiritual peace can flow in to heal our wounds and to lift our lives.

Finally, religion contributes to health through *the therapeutic value of worship and prayer*. In Shakespeare's *Hamlet,* as the watch at Elsinore waits for the ghost of Hamlet's father to appear, footsteps sound in the darkness. Recognizing them, Bernardo calls, "What! is Horatio there?" Horatio answers, "A piece of him."

Under the strain of modern living, most of us feel like Horatio; we become unraveled, disrupted and fragmented; we grow taut and excitable. Worship and prayer lead us into a different atmosphere. They take our tense bodies and feverish minds into the calm and quiet of the Eternal. Like the jewel merchant who looks away occasionally from the shining gems that the keenness of his vision may be sharpened to select the finest stone, so for a time we look away from the distracting scenes that we may discern the true, the beautiful and the good. Worship lifts and unifies our thoughts and emotions. It sets our lives in a fresh rhythm. It releases regenerative forces that add poise, sanity and insight in meeting the responsibilities which we face daily. Dr. Alexis Carrel wrote: "As a physician, I have seen men, after all other therapy had failed, lifted out of disease and melancholy by the serene effort of prayer. It is the only power in the world that seems to overcome the so-called 'Laws of nature'; the occasions on which prayer has dramatically done this have been termed 'miracles.' But a constant, quieter miracle takes place hourly in the hearts of men and women who have discovered that prayer supplies them with a steady flow of sustaining power in their daily lives." [3]

> In the castle of my soul
> Is a little postern gate,
> Whereat, when I enter,
> I am in the presence of God.
>
> . . . . .
>
> When I enter into God,
> All life has a meaning,
> Without asking I know;
> My desires are even now fulfilled,
> My fever is gone,
> In the great quiet of God.
> My troubles are but pebbles on the road,
> My joys are like the everlasting hills.
>
> . . . . .
>
> So it is when my soul steps through the postern gate
> Into the presence of God. [4]

An insight into the value of worship is suggested by the word itself. It comes from the Anglo-Saxon "weorthscipe"— "weorth" meaning "worth," and "scipe" meaning "ship." Thus worship is the practice of looking deep into the heart of things to discover their real worth. It is the quest for true value; it is untangling the enduring from the sham. In evaluating others, it is discerning the genuine and Godlike. In relation to God, it is opening our lives to Him to remove that which is crass and cheap, allowing Him to pull us together into new alignment. Worship fills us with renewed power and insight. Our wills and emotions, like spokes to the hub of a wheel, are centered around a purpose vital enough to command our deepest allegiance. The glory of life, it is well to remember, comes not from what we command but from what commands us; not from what we manipulate, but from what we reverence.

Some years ago the Archbishop of Canterbury, broadcasting a widely publicized message, declared that the world could be saved from political chaos by one thing only. That one thing, he affirmed, was worship. We might expect something as unrealistic as that from a clergyman, we tell ourselves ruefully. But before we condemn him as an addlepated idealist, quite detached from reality, let us examine his definition of worship. To him, worship meant "to quicken the conscience by the holiness of God; to feed the mind with the truth of God; to purge the imagination by the beauty of God; to open the heart to the love of God; and to devote the will to the purpose of God."

Conscience, mind, imagination, heart and will all directed to and centered in one mighty beneficent Power—consider what that would mean if applied to our lives. What priority is more urgent for our distracted world or our fragmented spirits? What greater boon could we grant our jaded emotions and jangled nerves? If with all our might we were to place our hearts, minds and wills systematically under the calming influence of worship and prayer, who can predict the curative effect?

These are suggestions as to ways in which religion aids health. The therapeutic value of such suggestions is nil, however, if they end when we finish with these pages. In order to help, they must become the basis of action. They have no practical value until we put them into practice. "If ye do . . . ye shall know. . . ."

> Lord, this hectic, fevered age
> Yearns for power to calm and cage
> Forces mad that through it rage
> And fill it with dismay.
>
> Rebels, we have kicked in scorn
> Stubbornly 'gainst goad and thorn:

Now at last, our strength o'erborne,
We cannot say thee nay.

Thou, O God, alone canst heal
Wounds of soul that from us steal
Hope and faith and steadfast zeal
And dim the light of day.

How great our need!—draw near to bless;
Speak thy clear word of holiness;
Wearied men to thee confess
Their longing for thy Way.

May thy grace surmount each ill,
May thy peace our pulses still,
May thy love uphold us till
Earth's shadows flee away.

NOTES

Scriptural quotations, unless otherwise indicated, are from the Authorized Version, and from the Revised Standard Version, published by Thomas Nelson & Sons, and copyright, 1946, by the Division of Christian Education of the National Council of the Churches of Christ in the United States of America.

Chapter I. Introduction to Happiness

1 Lillian Eichler Watson, ed., *Light from Many Lamps* (New York: Simon & Schuster, 1951), p. 12.
2 Herb Magidson and Ben Oakland, *Happiness.* Copyright, 1951, by George Simon, Inc. Used by permission.
3 *The Thoughts of Marcus Aurelius Antoninus,* translated by John Jackson (Oxford University Press, 1951), p. 14.
4 Joseph Auslander, "Badge of Courage," *This Week Magazine,* July 30, 1950. Used by permission.
5 Fritz Kunkel, *Let's Be Normal!* translated by Eleanore Jensen (New York: Ives Washburn, 1929), p. 212.
6 Alfred Adler, *The Practice and Theory of Individual Psychology,* translated by P. Padin (New York: Harcourt, Brace & Co., 1927). In the motivation of human personality, Dr. Adler places central "the will to prestige," or "the will to power." He conceives of the human personality as in competition with other personalities, the result being a struggle to get "on top" of every situation.
7 Gordon W. Allport, *Personality: A Psychological Interpretation* (New York: Henry Holt & Co., 1937), p. 213.

Chapter II. The Habit of Happiness

1 Richard C. Cabot, *What Men Live By* (Boston: Houghton Mifflin Co., 1914), pp. 17–18.
2 M. Arthur Kline, "We Are Born to Believe," in *Woman's Home Companion,* April, 1954.
3 C. S. Braden, "Why People Are Religious—A Study In Religious Motivation," *The Journal of Bible and Religion,* Jan., 1947, pp. 38–45.
4 J. A. Hadfield, *The Psychology of Power* (New York: The Macmillan Company, 1924), pp. 51–52.

Chapter III. Be Yourself

1 Channing Pollock, *The Fool* (New York: Brentano's, Inc., 1922), p. 38.
2 Carl G. Jung, *Contributions to Analytical Psychology,* translated by H.

243

G. and Cary F. Baynes (New York: Harcourt, Brace & Co., 1928), p. 384.

3 Cited in James Reid, *Facing Life with Christ* (Nashville, Cokesbury Press, 1940), pp. 101–2.

4 From the personal story of Mrs. Tillie Burkhardt, well-known caterer in St. Louis, Mo., on *This I Believe,* presented by Edward R. Murrow in 1954.

Chapter IV. Faith and Happiness

1 Elizabeth York Case, "There Is No Unbelief."

Chapter V. Where the "Practical" Man Loses Out

1 Sam Walter Foss, "The Two Gods," from *Songs of the Average Man* by Sam Walter Foss. Used by permission of Lothrop, Lee & Shepard Co., Inc.

Chapter VI. Making the Most of Our Abilities

1 Eve Curie, *Madame Curie,* translated by Vincent Sheean (New York: Doubleday & Company, 1938), pp. 175–77.

2 Marcus Aurelius Antoninus, in Jackson, *op. cit.,* Bk. V, Sec. 16.

3 Whitney Bolton, *The Silver Spade* (New York: Farrar, Straus & Young, 1954), pp. vii–viii.

4 A. J. Cronin, "The Turning Point of My Career," in *The Reader's Digest,* May, 1941, pp. 53–57.

Chapter VII. The Art of Living Together

1 A. S. M. Hutchinson, *This Freedom* (Boston, Little, Brown & Co., 1922), p. 229.

2 *Plato,* translated by B. Jowett, edited by Louis Ropes Loomis (New York: Walter J. Black, 1942), pp. 178–80.

Chapter VIII. Managing Our Moods

1 Sydney J. Harris, "Strictly Personal," in *The Chicago Daily News.* Used by permission.

2 Hesketh Pearson, *G.B.S.: A Full Length Portrait* (New York: Harper & Brothers, 1942), p. 29.

Chapter IX. Mastering Our Resentments

1 Cited in James Gordon Gilkey, *You Can Master Your Life* (New York: The Macmillan Company, 1934), pp. 82–83.

2 Frances Winwar, *The Immortal Lovers* (New York: Harper & Brothers, 1950), pp. 32–40.

3 "The Disease of Resentment," in *Democracy in Action,* February, 1953, pp. 1–3. Used by permission.

Chapter X. Overcoming Our Anxieties

1 Cited in David Seabury, *Help Yourself to Happiness* (New York: McGraw-Hill, 1937), p. 150.

2 Gilkey, *op. cit.*, p. 26.

Chapter XI. When Trouble Troubles Us

1 Marcus Aurelius Antoninus, in Jackson, *op. cit.*
2 Harold Russell and Victor Rosen, *Victory in My Hands* (New York: Creative Press, 1949), pp. 278–80.
3 Ella Wheeler Wilcox, "The Winds of Fate" (New York: W. B. Conkey Co.). Used by permission.
4 George Seaver, *Edward Wilson of the Antarctic* (London: J. Murray Company, 1933), chap. 11.

Chapter XII. Laughter Is Holy, Too

1 Albert Schweitzer, "Religion in Modern Civilization," in *The Christian Century,* November 21 and 28, 1934.

Chapter XIII. The Conquest of Suffering

1 Cited in Elbert Russell, *The Beatitudes* (New York: Harper & Brothers, 1929), p. 43.
2 Eugene O'Neill, "All God's Children," *Nine Plays* (New York: Liveright, Inc., 1932), Act 2, Sc. 2.
3 Antony Alpers, *Katherine Mansfield: A Biography* (New York: Alfred A. Knopf, 1953), p. 310.
4 Lincoln Barnett, "God and the American People," in *Ladies' Home Journal,* November, 1948.
5 George Matheson, "O Love That Will Not Let Me Go." Used by permission of Novello & Company, Ltd., London.

Chapter XIV. Religion, Health and Happiness

1 Gotthard Booth, "Health from the Standpoint of the Physician," in *The Church and Mental Health,* edited by Paul B. Maves (New York: Charles Scribner's Sons, 1953), p. 9.
2 Marcus Aurelius Antoninus, in Jackson, *op. cit.* In similar vein he writes (pp. 25–26): "In the mind of a man who has been chastened and purified, thou wilt find no festering wounds, no uncleanness, no treacherous sores. . . . In such a man, moreover, there is nothing servile and nothing affected: he is neither bound up with others or altogether divorced from them; nor in his conduct is there aught that need fear scrutiny or hide itself from the light of day."
3 Alexis Carrel, "Prayer Is Power," in *The Reader's Digest,* March, 1941, p. 34.
4 Walter Rauschenbusch, "The Little Gate to God."

Set in Linotype Caledonia
Format by Edwin H. Kaplin
Manufactured by The Haddon Craftsmen, Inc.
Published by HARPER & BROTHERS, *New York*